The Heretics: Past and Present

Can We Now Explain the Unexplainable?

The Heretics: Past and Present

Can We Now Explain the Unexplainable?

Brian Allan

BOOKS

Winchester, UK
Washington, USA

First published by O-Books, 2010
O Books is an imprint of John Hunt Publishing Ltd., The Bothy, Deershot Lodge, Park Lane, Ropley, Hants, SO24 0BE, UK
office1@o-books.net
www.o-books.com

For distributor details and how to order please visit the 'Ordering' section on our website.

ISBN: 978 1 84694 309 6

A CIP catalogue record for this book is available from the British Library.

Design: Tom Davies

Printed in the UK by CPI Antony Rowe
Printed in the USA by Offset Paperback Mfrs, Inc

We operate a distinctive and ethical publishing philosophy in all areas of its business, from its global network of authors to production and worldwide distribution.

CONTENTS

Acknowledgments

I wish to thank my colleague, Mr Malcolm Robinson, the founder of Strange Phenomena Investigations (SPI), for information relating to a device invented by Mr. Tony Bassett who is one of the people mentioned in Chapter Twenty Eight of this book. I also wish to express appreciation and thanks to Mr Ellis Taylor for sage advice and to the ever-resourceful Mr Philip Gardiner for opening doors. Finally as always, my love and appreciation go to my dear wife Ann, who, as always, gives inspiration and unswerving loyalty.

Introduction

This book is intended to allow you, the seeker into occult lore as practiced in recent times and other related subjects that still create much heated debate, to peer through the cracks in the façade of normality that has, over time, been constructed to conceal many dark and frequently uneasy truths concerning the human condition. Doing so deserves some timely words of warning and caution therefore you should consider your position very carefully. At one stage in the history of our race your natural curiosity would have automatically condemned you as a heretic and your route to official salvation, (if it was even offered) would have been short, brutal and frequently agonizing. It is curious to learn that salvation and forgiveness frequently equated with death and your path to a hypothetical pardon was often glimpsed through the flames engulfing you at the stake. While there are currently no official proscriptions denying the natural instinct of curiosity, you should keep firmly in mind that history is cyclical, and because of this humanity, in spite of all its abundant talent, is almost guaranteed through inherent stupidity, pride, greed and arrogance to repeat its mistakes.

This book is presented in four sections; the first suggests that there is complete interchangeability between magic, the occult and religion, and in spite of continuous repudiations and denials we find that these subjects tread similar paths and in the past have even worn the same shoes. All religions from the very earliest times were founded on a 'revelation' in one form or another made to an individual and this revelation was usually from what is considered to be an 'angel' or other supernatural being. Is it likely that these wondrous entities had no heavenly provenance whatsoever, and both they and their agendas may have originated in some murky and far off, invisible *'otherworld'*? Could this entity have been one of the beings also allegedly unleashed in comparatively recent times by such magicians as Aleister Crowley and Jack Parsons and indeed, are they still among us?

In bygone eras for example is it not strange that the prophet Mohammed encountered an 'angel', Gabriel, from who he learned the precepts of Islam, or many centuries later that Joseph Smith, the founder of Mormonism, had a very similar encounter with an 'angelic' being called Moroni? In both cases the precious metal, gold, was involved, Gabriel presented Mohammed with a 'golden tablet' commanding him to read it and Moroni gave Joseph Smith 'magical spectacles' called *'Urim and Thummim'*, with which to translate texts written in an unknown language called 'reformed Egyptian', these texts were also written on 'golden plates'. Why specifically gold? Was this because its intrinsic value implied great wealth and gave the story greater significance, or might it have been a factor of the electrical properties of the metal? Does this hint at the possibility that properties inherent in magic and the occult may be a factor of the electromagnetic spectrum? An even earlier instance of initiation comes from the mystery school of *'Manichaeism'*. In this case, at the age of twelve the founder, Mani, encountered a being that he referred to as *'The Twin'*. This being imparted a great secret, which revealed that evil had continually influenced the human race and that there was a continual battle throughout the cosmos between the opposing forces of good and evil.

This mystery school was quite widespread and even counted St Augustine among its many initiates. Another apparent connection between the early church and magic involves Bishop Clement of Alexandria, who taught his advanced students what he called the 'disciplina arcani' (*lit. secret disciplines*), which were, in effect, magical practices and techniques. Curiously enough this supposed cosmic battle finds a strange resonance in claims from sections within the UFO community suggesting that there is a battle currently raging in the cosmos concerning the takeover of planet Earth and its inhabitants. In this scenario a race known as 'The Nordics', (who seem to conform to the western angelic stereotype being attractive, tall, blue-eyed blondes), are on the side of humanity, while enemy have all the characteristics of demons etc typified by images of grays and reptilians. Oddly enough, the reader will find several synchronous crossovers between magic, religion and Ufology as they progress through the chapters of this book; is this by accident or design, or perhaps do the era, culture and context define reality? Magic and magical beliefs in the form of animism existed long before religion and, in spite of religion's best efforts to stifle them, they have continued to exist in parallel and will, in spite of everything, continue to exist; one must ask oneself why? One must also ask why has a considerable sum of money has been spent by various government agencies all over the world attempting to harness 'magical' forces for their own purposes. Is this possible, is this practical, or is it something that only exists in the tales of wizardry created by writers of fantasy fiction.

The second section looks at this very issue and suggests that some writers may even have succeeded in breaching the gateways, reaching into worlds that exist beside our own. In other words, as with many instances involving the occult, the only difference between fantasy and reality lies in the perspective of the observer. Might the horrors the writers envisioned actually exist in some altered reality and gradually drip-feed into their subconscious minds to find a type of specious existence in the written word. Or more worryingly, might the very act of reading about them in some way alter the neural processes of the reader and present them with the chance to materialize in our world? Is their malign presence the influence behind the serial killers and multiple rapists who prey on society? Or are the tales simply words of warning about dimensional entities whose potential for hatred and malice is unknowable? As you will see, throughout this section the distinct imprint of occult and magical lore permeates its very fibres.

Section Three reveals opinions from various sources concerning the appearance of the human race here on Earth. How did we get here and could our moon have provided the means to do so, or was there another method? We find bizarre experiments to recreate the very essence of life and even claims that a strange form of life was created, apparently artificially, during the mid 19th century. Was Darwin right or did he fail to grasp a much bigger picture simply because the idea required was just too vast and the prevailing science was just not up to proving it? As you will discover, the instinctive and repressive influence of religion tried to stifle his breakthroughs and to some extent still does, indeed Creationism casts a long, long shadow and still flourishes in the American 'bible belt'.

Finally, in Section Four we consider whether or not science has come a step too far. Does the fact that we *can* do something mean that we actually *should* do it, or are there some areas of research best left alone? Has our race evolved as far as it can or is the future already here, just waiting in the wings until the conditions are right for it to emerge? One thing linking all of these seemingly disparate issues is the subject that opened this book, the pale, twin specters of magic and religion, but they now seem to find expression in a number of much more subtle and diverse guises. There is however hope, for although what is revealed in these pages may not exactly induce peace of mind, it just might sow the need for a greater understanding of what is real and what is not and in that search for knowledge the seeker might find the source of their own salvation. Since to some extent we choose our own road in life and the vehicle in which to travel, we should choose wisely.

~

Section One

The Magicians

~

Chapter One
The Roots of Occult Belief

The occult, magic, Satanism, devil worship and all that these entail, have in the main been with us in one form or another almost since the beginning of time, and initially at least they were regarded as simple if powerful tools with which our ancient ancestors sought to control and make sense of the forces, natural and otherwise, that beset them. Gradually, with the slow onset of civilization, these practices were gradually adapted as the people using them also evolved and learned. Eventually the customs and rituals were formalized, and through a steady process beginning with animism and nature worship, slowly morphed, for good or ill, into the many strands and variants of religion that currently exist today. Unfortunately, what we now consider as 'enlightened beliefs' brought with them a degree of intolerance, ignorance and hatred that is scarcely credible to any fair-minded person, negative and hateful qualities that are still prevalent throughout the world to the present day.

The original faiths were polytheistic, meaning that they necessitated the worship of a varying number of Gods, each assuming whatever role the particular culture thought appropriate. I should make it clear that I shall in the main, although by no means exclusively, refer to Christianity throughout the introduction and indeed the rest of the book, because that is the belief system which is most relevant in the west and also the one which seems the most amenable to change in outlook. The fact that Christianity is still capable of change and revision has, in comparison with the inflexibility of other beliefs, perhaps been one of the factors in its survival since it first appeared, although some might argue that this will eventually lead to its extinction. As an aside, it may even be arguable that Roman Catholicism, which is the truly great and original variant on Christian belief, still contains some elements of polytheism in the triumvirate of the 'Holy Trinity' – the Father, the Son (or should that be the Sun?) and the Holy Spirit. This is in addition to the worship and adoration of Mary, the Mother of Christ, also referred to as *'The Queen of Heaven'* and the panoply of saints that inhabit the celestial hierarchy of the faithful. Although they cannot completely eradicate it, the hierarchy of the Catholic Church treats the veneration and cult of Mary with considerable suspicion if not outright hostility. It is also fair to say that it was the veneration of the saints and the creation of images in their likeness that lead to charges of idolatry from the early Protestant Church, which in turn was considered heretical by the Roman Church.

Quite naturally such a concept was roundly rejected and condemned by the Church, which produced reams of closely reasoned arguments and rationalizations to justify its official view on the matter. As far as the Church was (and still is) concerned, the Trinity was a mystical/magical concept encompassing three entities in the one body, so that when Jesus walked the earth it was as an extension of God Himself, Jesus was an Avatar, a God manifesting as a human being and displaying some of His powers. Another aspect of the Catholic faith that causes much concern and deep mistrust in non-Catholic faiths is the concept of *'Transubstantiation'*, where Christ actually manifests, albeit spiritually, on the altar during the sacrament of Holy Communion. It is perhaps the main stumbling block to any form of unity or ecumenism between the various shades of belief on the Christian palette and is the closest that we will ever come to public displays of officially sanctioned 'magic'.

Reinforcement of doctrine comes partly through a measure of

sheer apathy and inertia and not a little fear on the part of the faithful, because to challenge the underpinnings of one's own belief can cause deep personal unease. This being the case it is usually left to outsiders and those of little or no faith to rock the sturdy boat of orthodoxy, and from any conventional viewpoint it is they who are considered 'damned'. Damned perhaps, but nowadays not candidates for overt persecution and even execution, which is precisely what orthodox Islam threatens those brave or foolish enough to challenge what is written in the Qur'an, or even worse, to actually leave the Islamic faith and adopt another. At its most extreme and literalist, those who are adjudged guilty of apostasy by an Islamic court are regarded as fair game to be murdered for their choice and indeed if the state cannot fulfill this injunction it is the duty of devout Muslims to carry out the act.

The very concept of heresy under Islamic (or, more correctly, Sharia) rule should be almost impossible since Muslims regards themselves as the property or slaves of Allah *(ibaad Allah)* and have submitted themselves body and soul to the law of God as set out in the Qur'an; they are therefore, literally, His possessions. From an Islamic point of view to leave Islam is to leave Allah (*the 'owner'*) and consequently is regarded as theft. This in turn weakens the Islamic state and is regarded as an act of revolt. According to Sharia law the guilty party is to be taken forcibly into custody and persuaded (by torture if necessary) to return to the fold. If the person is sufficiently strong willed or committed enough and the persuasion and coercion fails, then the Sharia says that the person must be executed by the state.

Yet still there are Islamic heretics, although in this case the context is vastly different, Sunni and Shia, the two great and apparently irreconcilable divisions within Islam, regard one another as apostates and heretics, hence the continuing state of undeclared war between the two schisms. It is unlikely that they will allow the differences to heal anytime soon, although in times of hardship (or war) the two divergent views join together as one for mutual protection. Incidentally, unlike other beliefs Islam permits no images of its deity, Allah, on the grounds that such an image would automatically be flawed because Allah represents absolute perfection and any attempt to reproduce such a being would be impossible and intolerable due to the inherent imperfection of mankind.

Now, sadly, extremism has found an outlet in Afghanistan where agents of the fundamentalist Taleban, aided and abetted by Al-Qaida cells, try to cling on to what they regard as theirs, where they can impose their harsh interpretation of Islam on the entire country. Although held temporarily in check, the bleak and mountainous nature of the country makes their decisive overthrow almost impossible. The British have been there three times since the 19th century and failed, the Russians with their vast military resources tried unsuccessfully for years to dislodge them when they were called the *Mujihadeen* (or those that wage Jihad or Holy War). This word is sometimes rendered as *Mujahideen* due to the frequently phonetic nature of transcribing Arabic into English, but the meanings are identical.

This is of course not to say that Islam, and Judaism for that matter, are not without their heretics and/or free thinkers, indeed some of the most influential ancient treatises on alternative belief were written in Hebrew and Arabic script. These include those who chose to act against traditional teaching, because the fact that Jesus Christ was a Jew who rebelled against his faith and created his own version of 'the truth' is conveniently ignored, and that he was viewed as a heretic and therefore according the laws of Judaism 'damned', even more so. One of the other curious aspects of Christian belief is the adoption of Jesus Christ as the true name of the founder of the faith that carries His name for it is not. The given name of this individual was Yeoshua (*Yeshua or Joshua*) ben Yoseph; a literal translation of this would be *'Yeoshua, son of Joseph'* and the use of the name, Christ, only denotes *'savior'*. An exact parallel of this is also found in the Islamic world where a person will have the word, 'Ibn', as part of their name and it too means 'son of'. 'Ibn' or 'ben', there is not too much difference in the English spelling and each show the influences of both the Hebrew and Arabic language.

Among Jews who were specifically accused of heresy are such names as *Korach,* whom the Talmud condemns as a heretic. He is joined by *Shabbsthai Zvi,* a false messiah who converted to Islam, *Benedict Spinoza* who was excommunicated for his pantheistic teachings and also *Maimonides* whose written works were condemned and burned to stop the spread of his heretical opinions. In the UK, due to his published ideas, Rabbi *Louis Jacobs* was branded a heretic and stopped from becoming the British Chief Rabbi. He was also removed from his synagogue much as a disgraced priest or minister would be removed their church. Whatever the differences these people had with their original faiths, none of them actually went as far as rejecting the concept of an omnipresent and omnipotent God somewhere in the background; the differences came in how, in their opinions, that particular God should be worshipped.

In earlier times gods fulfilling the same function frequently went by different names depending on whether the culture was based on Mayan, Aztec, Roman, Syrian, Greek, Egyptian, Celtic or indeed any given belief. The unifying factor was the fact that each civilization required acceptance of some force greater than itself to invoke, praise or condemn, depending on what event had occurred. A fundamental example of this is found in sun worship where the Sun was regarded as a deity in its own right and in certain South American cultures had to be appeased by regular human sacrifice to ensure that it returned from the pit of darkness that arrived when it plunged over the horizon on its regular cycle of day and night.

Although not entirely confined to the practices of the Aztecs and the other mainly southern civilizations, the magical concept of death and renewal became inextricably linked with the sun, an idea that sustained the mainly Roman worship of the god, Mithras, which was a direct development of earlier sun worship. This in turn led to the cult of *'Sol Invictus'*, or the *'Invincible Sun'* and it is persuasively argued that belief in Jesus Christ shares the same basic premise as the dying and rising god. In a direct allegory of sunrise and sunset; Christ, we are told, died for our sins but was reborn to lead us to salvation; it may be the very reason that he came to be called *'The Son of Man'* and the spelling of 'son' rather than 'sun' is not accidental. It should also be emphasized that in common with its forbears, Mithraism also had many ritual elements that were magical/occult in nature.

As we shall see, to even discuss deviations from orthodoxy such as those above might constitute sufficient grounds to label the person offering them as a heretic and therefore damned, and we shall return to this subject very shortly. However, what has been mentioned here is almost ephemeral, the most gentle of zephyrs compared to the raging tempest of rejection and denial of what comes later in this book; and this only refers to religious damnation, because we shall also consider what happens to those who reject the orthodoxy of mainstream science. Even here it is difficult to keep the icy and controlling hand of religion out of the equation, because the unthinking dogma of faith reaches into these hallowed cloisters of logic and reason. Leaving aside the near disaster that befell both Copernicus and Galileo when they dared to challenge what the Catholic Church proclaimed as 'the truth', a similar influence exists today although to a considerably lesser degree. However, a much more severe fate awaited the Greek philosopher, Socrates, who questioned the polytheistic teachings of his era and was sentenced by the courts in Athens to be burned at the stake.

It is important to appreciate that the founders and patriarchs of all three monotheistic faiths were, in their way, regarded as heretics and not just those that have emerged since, although, as always, context is the vital mark of separation. Jesus was accused a heretic by the Sanhedrin, or Jewish high council, and aged 33 was handed over to the occupying Romans for sentence and execution. The choice of the term, heretic, as applied to Christ is in itself very interesting and bizarre: originally Christ was regarded as a trouble maker and political agitator, but unfortunately for his accusers neither 'crime' deserved the death penalty let alone crucifixion. To guarantee his death, Christ was actually accused of being a *'malificus'*, which can be translated as 'magician', and this was the crime warranting death by crucifixion. The Islamic prophet, Mohammed, was accused of a dangerous heresy by questioning the old Islamic traditions of slavery, usury, racism and xenophobia, and even the Jewish prophet, Abraham, was thrown into the fiery furnace for his heresy, although God immediately saved him – miracle, magic or something entirely different?

The fledgling Christian faith and its promoters, while maintaining an outwardly stern and unyielding outlook towards the earlier beliefs, was still not strong enough to spread its version of 'the truth' by force of arms and of necessity developed a stoic pragmatism. They understood that where there was going to be a revolt against their teachings it was much easier to simply subsume the particular divergent practice into the canon of its own teachings. Once accepted it could be either be conveniently forgotten, or if not forgotten then molded and adapted to suit the churches own ends. This was mutually beneficial to all parties, the church got new members with little dissent and as a result grew stronger, while the practitioners of the older belief perhaps found their lives improved and enriched through access to better facilities of all kinds. This happy situation later changed markedly as the Church, because of its pre-eminence in society, could enforce its will by sheer might alone.

The 'old ways' were the precursors to what later became better understood as 'magic', and although officially denounced and proscribed by all faiths that purport to worship a creator God, the subject attracted many of the curious within the orthodoxy of Judaism and Christianity, and of course a few centuries later, Islam, although as we have seen, Islamic heretics were considerably more circumspect in their opinions. One of the earliest examples of the appearance of the 'old ways' within Judaism was in the construction of Solomon's temple when King Solomon - allegedly – in addition to employing 80,000 stonemasons etc, manifested a total of forty demons to assist in the construction of his Temple. It should come as no surprise to learn that King Solomon was regarded as a demonologist of some note.

As we shall discover, the practice of consorting with demons and the other denizens of Hell was also a preoccupation of a few of the early patriarchs of the Roman Catholic Church. It is interesting to note that along with King Solomon, no one associated with the hierarchy of any of the faiths, whether monotheistic or otherwise, is considered to be 'damned' through their meddling with the so-called forces of darkness; but as always it rather depends of the context and who is making the rules in the first place. It cannot be the purposes that such dangerous liaisons are designed to achieve, for the great and good were just as tempted and lead astray as the most irreligious dabbler in the practice of magic and conjuration. It seems as if the old saying that, "It's the rich that gets the pleasure and the poor that gets the blame", has been around for a very long time indeed.

In addition to magic, and the practice of magic as we shall also see, it is not the only way to find oneself damned, because to believe in something that is not in any way associated with magic, yet challenges the accepted dogma and orthodoxy of science and religion, can also result in the classification of whomever holds these beliefs as an 'outsider', a heretic who, by their act of rebellion, is automatically damned. In fact the origins of the word 'heretic' have no apparent relationship to its eventual association with spiritual ruin and rejection of the 'true faith'. All the word means is, literally, *'one who chooses'*. So the mere act of deciding for oneself what is true and acceptable automatically separates one from the rump of orthodoxy, whether this be religious, scientific or any other branch of the 'official truth'. For this reason this book examines some of these avenues and choices, everything from magic, magicians and even authors, through the origins of the human race, to the outer limits of UFOs and those who almost deify them. Hopefully by the time you have read this book to the end you will see that there are tangible links between these apparently diverse subjects, links that irrevocably bind us together.

Unfortunately it also becomes increasingly clear that in this politically correct quagmire we currently wade through there is a constant danger of upsetting many disparate factions who choose to believe that theirs is the only truth, that there is a divine ruler, a God that oversees and ultimately judges (and in some cases justifies) every aspect of their lives. This is still manifest today in the irrational dogma associated with some evangelical and fundamentalist Christian schisms who are absolutely certain that everyone except them are condemned to burn in the fires of Hell. As far as they are concerned the reason is quite simple: according to scripture Christ said that *'the only way to the Father is through me'*. There is no room for error or deviation here; if you do not accept Christ as your savior then you are automatically damned, a hopeless reject ultimately condemned to suffer and die.

This of course means that, logically, all the billions of people who existed before (and for that matter after) Christ, all of the Jews, Muslims, Hindu's, Buddhists, Jains, Wiccan's, animists, non-believers, and all the rest who have lived otherwise blameless and decent lives will see no reward for their efforts. This heartless, arid and contradictory version of traditional Christian teachings demonstrates that the core values of peace, love and tolerance are meaningless within its dogma. It also clearly shows that damnation is closer than some people care to believe, and that perhaps the soulless bigots who ascribe to this desiccated view may find themselves judged and found wanting. It is also unfortunate that many of those who hold this opinion live in America and have the ear of many movers and shakers in government; people like the Rev. Jerry Falwell, Rev. Pat Robertson and more recently pastor John Hagee. All of them are evangelicals and in the case of Falwell and Robertson, well-known right-wing 'televangelists' who still preach over the airwaves alternately praising the Lord and raising money for their cause. Hagee is much the same and regularly warns that Armageddon is at hand and only the faithful will be saved from the cataclysm during the 'Rapture'.

When this event, which, in spite of clear magical overtones is not regarded by its followers as in any way occult occurs, only the true believers will be bodily lifted from the Earth's surface to reside with God until the forces of Christ have won the planet-wide battle against the Anti-Christ and Satan. The rapture will no doubt cause much inconvenience to the remaining population as aircraft, cars, trucks and trains crash when those of the true believers controlling them are 'raptured' and disappear, and surgeons vanish during operations – you get the picture? Evidently the sequence of events begins when Russia, in league with surrounding Islamic nations, attacks Israel, but Israel is by some miracle spared and the invaders crushed. This is followed by a seven year 'tribulation', when the Antichrist convinces all nations that he is the only way forward and then, joined by the 'false prophet', he destroys all opposition to create a single world government, which is surely the 'New World Order' much trumpeted by conspiracy theorists.

The antichrist is then assassinated by two Jews, but is restored to life by Satan Himself (magic or an application of technology?), which only serves to demonstrate to any waverers just how powerful and omnipotent He is. Finally, armies from Russia and China are deployed against Him, which is odd considering that

Russia originally attacked Israel, but he manages to talk them into changing allegiance and supporting Him and this combined might is hurled at Israel. Fortunately, by this time Christ has returned with an army of angels to soundly defeat the Antichrist and the 'false prophet', and with the battle now in the bag for forces of light the believers will be returned to Earth to live in peace and harmony for the next thousand years. Presumably at this point the Earth will be inhabited by an exclusively Christian population, the rest having been killed during the war.

Strange, terrifying even, but true, these are beliefs of the fundamentalist individuals whose word is unquestioningly believed by hundreds of thousands of people, perhaps even millions, in the United States of America and elsewhere. Are we the damned or are they? Hopefully as this book progresses we will be able to come to an answer and as we shall see, these beliefs are no stranger then some we will encounter; in fact they make some of them look quite ordinary and 'run of the mill'. It shows in no uncertain manner that religion, as well as a supernatural force for good, is, equally, a force of great evil and source of damnation its own right. This account also seems to further corroborate the ideology behind the hypothetical and probably insoluble conflict between good and evil whether this is presented in a traditional sense or that promoted via the UFO community. Furthermore, this group also has schools of thought (admittedly on the outer edges) insisting that the human race will be lifted from the planet in a fleet of gigantic spacecraft, which even now are 'cloaked' and parked in the void.

It is unfortunate that this should be the case, but as I continue to investigate the roots of humanity and its beliefs, it becomes blatantly obvious that there are some aspects of the human condition that defy explanation except in terms of what we have, in our ignorance, chosen to label 'supernatural'. This description has perhaps inevitably become interwoven with religion, because religion itself is by its very nature and definition also 'supernatural'. In spite of the protestations by the faithful, often backed unquestioningly by scientists who should know better, there is clear and slowly mounting evidence that we are the sole masters of our own destiny and, literally, the creators of our own future. The concept of 'the supernatural' does, I suspect, cause the doctrine and dogma makers of all faiths considerable introspection and no little fear, because they have to define what is acceptable and unacceptable when faced with certain phenomena. As we have already seen, these phenomena may serve to place them outside what is considered normal, although this may not be too great a hindrance since in many cases they 'move the goalposts' to suit by changing the interpretation of the source material itself.

For example, a 'miracle' (again magic by a more theologically acceptable name) is judged appropriate when, after suitable scrutiny, it is decided that it occurred or was brought about by the application of approved methods such as prayer to God, or, in Roman Catholic belief, one of the many saints canonized by the Roman Catholic Church. If, however, such an event was judged to have been caused by a non-approved agency, e.g. a faith healer or worse still a psychic medium, then there is every chance that it would adjudged the work of some unholy agency, probably demonic in nature. It would never occur to the inquisitors that the miracle had been brought about by the mere act of wishing for it to happen; admitting to such a possibility would have, in their eyes, the horrific overtones that we are in effect gods in our own right. We literally create the present and the future by our own actions and desires; we are in a very real sense at one with the planet and indeed the universe itself. This was understood millennia ago by other philosophers, faiths and beliefs, long before the monotheistic faiths evolved from a series of visionaries, prophets and shamans.

The many other systems of belief and enlightenment, although possessed of one basic understanding of the unity of the physical and the metaphysical, still had to deify what is inextricably locked and encoded into each and every one of who has ever lived or will ever live. This being the case, I wish to make clear from the outset that what follows is not an attack on religion or belief; people are, quite correctly and providing it is not harmful or dangerous, absolutely free to accept as true whatever they are comfortable with. What is presented here is a dispassionate evaluation of belief, not in scripture, although at a few junctures I quote from it to make a point, but in the alternatives that have been put forward to allow people to understand the visible and invisible world around them. This of course relies entirely on faith, which is rather deftly summed up in the following quote from the author, physicist and director of the Origin Initiative at Arizona State University, Lawrence Krause; "Faith lies in the realm of human activity that has little to do with reason. For most people religion is one way of making sense of an irrational world, a world that is not fair, in which human justice is an afterthought". This astute observation resonates well with what I have already said about our ancestors harnessing whatever they could to control or understand the world around them; the only difference is that by implication it refers to a more modern era.

It is unavoidable that religion is involved in this evaluation because, for good or ill, what is written in the Bible (and the Talmud and the Qur'an) is still accepted as an absolute and irrevocable fact by enormous numbers of people the world over. Another area covered in these pages is the very real possibility that what we have traditionally come to regard as 'magic', or the ability to make things happen just by deciding that we want them to, is also a reality and is a long forgotten aspect of ancient technology. Stranger still, perhaps it ceased to function merely because we stopped believing that it would. This a concept used to good effect in the original series of 'Star Trek' in a rather poignant 1966 episode entitled, *'Who Mourns for Adonis'*, where the last of the ancient Greek Gods, in this case Apollo, was shown to be an entity that only existed because people worshipped and, crucially, believed in him. In this episode Adonis explains that the rest of the gods had gradually died of loneliness and literally faded away. As far as he was concerned the more people believed and praised him the greater his power became. The episode ended, predictably, with the god vanishing when the crew of the Enterprise refused to accept his divinity and would not worship him. The lure was there, it was almost a form of symbiosis: in return for their adoration Adonis would supply all their physical needs and requirements; but the crew would have none of it. Yes, this was a work of fiction but the rationale is identical.

There are in this world some subjects and people who, for one reason or another, create a very real aura of unease and fear around them. They seem to attract ill fortune like magnets, and those who choose to associate with them do so almost in the instinctive manner of moths drawn into a deadly flirtation with a naked flame. Why then are these issues so apparently irresistible? Is it because they represent a sense of rebellion and freedom from convention, a lonely voice shouting against the implacable thunder of normality, or, depending on the nature of the issue, an attempt to wrap oneself in what they represent? Does the person so doing believe that, by association, they render themselves invulnerable to run-of-the-mill matters that bedevil and beset the rest of society? It may be that the seekers after gnosis are genuinely looking for enlightenment and hidden knowledge or, equally, is it the sheer charisma of the 'teacher' sufficient? This apparent dichotomy may be resolved in the following chapters.

Chapter 2
The Damned

There is more than one definition of those individuals who are, for one reason or another, considered 'damned', or in some other way in the throes of perdition. In some cases this has occurred because they were, in its purest sense 'Gnostics', or those merely seeking 'gnosis' or spiritual knowledge; but in many instances where this has been the case their quest has run afoul of the authorities, invariably the Church. This definition is traditional and reflects the days when the Christian, i.e. Roman Catholic Church ruled unchallenged in Europe and its edicts were law; because at the time there was no separation between church and state and because the state drew its authority directly from the Church, the ecclesiastics were always hovering in the background like puppet masters pulling the strings. It is vital to appreciate that Gnosticism in the shape of *'mystery schools'* of one kind or another was present even prior to the creation of the Christian church, and indeed to some extent still is, although over the centuries with the introduction of improved standards of education and a measure of democracy this has gradually eroded.

It is a situation that has to some extent been aided and abetted by the seemingly inexorable, long, slow, implosion of the Church due to internal schisms, apathy, politics, corruption and other issues. Although hailed as a type of liberation, this state of affairs may be far from desirable since, if nothing else, a united Church provided a rock of certainty to cling to and its values inspired, and also to some extent enforced, social cohesion and structure.

Although it has to be said that some fundamentalist Christians from the ragged edges of acceptability, especially in the United States of America, have periodically created their own enclosed 'micro worlds' run on literalist biblical lines. This utopian type of environment is all well and good, but serves those who lead and live it very badly because it only reinforces their unthinking belief that they and their source of inspiration, the Bible, are right. They apparently fail to accept and understand that they are only able to live their idealized life though tolerance and the decidedly non-religious and non-sacred protection of the American military machine.

Unfortunately, the religious basis underpinning the Constitution of the USA and the guarantees it contains to some extent encourage and rationalize such displays of independence, which in many cases, regrettably, end in failure, imprisonment and in some extreme cases death; the Waco fiasco is a case in point. Likewise it has also been argued that the insidious undermining of religious beliefs and values has encouraged a corresponding growth of a ghetto-like culture in societal values and it may even be in the public interest to live by strictly enforced guidelines even when they do not appear to be fair. However, as we have seen, some countries in the Middle East where there is an Islamic hegemony and what is in effect a theocratic dictatorship, apply *'Sharia Law'*, which is based on the Qur'an and is part and parcel of the civil process that forms the basis for day-to-day life and the legislation that governs it.

Here, due to self-regulating internal and external strictures, the system appears to work; but Gnosticism is not obvious. If it does exist it is in the utmost secrecy because any attempt to usurp the religious status quo is dealt with in the severest terms, and independent thought contrary to what is contained in the Suras of Qur'an and its Hadiths (commentaries) is absolutely proscribed. One of the very few examples of what might be regarded as a type of overt *'Islamic Gnosticism'* is the practice of

'Sufism', which is a mystical branch of Islam dedicated to meditation and personal contact with God. This is a definition that also encompasses those who subscribe to the Dervish school of asceticism, which is normally associated with an ecstatic whirling dance designed to produce altered states of awareness and trance states.

What these beliefs do not do however is, unlike Christian Gnosticism, question Islamic orthodoxy. It is not up to me to act as a judge regarding how these lifestyles function or indeed their effectiveness, but even a casual observer can today look around and see how, in the absence of morality or ethics learned from either religious sources or the family unit, the state becomes the arbiter of what is or is not permissible. This has lead to a steady build up in the control, monitoring and surveillance of the everyday lives of the people who live in any given country; perhaps it is more visible in the United Kingdom because it is relatively small and racially diverse, but it is present to some degree everywhere.

This is, of course, not to say that one system is good and the other is not, it is merely designed to demonstrate that even today there are wide theological and cultural divisions in what is considered as acceptable or normal. However, for the sake of simplicity and although as already stated I will attempt to remove any religious pressures and constraints from the equation, it is almost inevitable that they will occur, because in the cases we will consider, those involved railed against established beliefs and dogmas and searched for alternatives. Because of this we will examine some of those who, by their lifestyle, inclination and rejection of the established order effectively rendered themselves outsiders, and whose views created – and still create – ripples of unease in the darker corners of the human psyche. Chief among this fairly exotic group of people are those of a creative bent, writers, poets, painters, self-styled magicians and others, including musicians, whose pursuits took them outside conventional ways of dealing with the strictures of the societies in which they lived. Once again it is almost inevitable that this group should include a sizeable number of those who have chosen to reject orthodox religion and beat their own paths.

In fact they more or less condemned themselves to this state due to a near visceral need for gnosis and/or iconoclasm in one manner or another, although it is probably fair to say that the less than liberal social and cultural mores of the times in which they lived had a great deal to do with their isolation. Of the more memorable are such diverse personalities as the notorious magicians, Aleister Edward Crowley (1875-1947), Anton Szandor LaVey (1924-1997), Kenneth Grant (1924-), and Austin Osman Spare (1886-1956); there are many, many more, but these four are perhaps among the best known. Others whose literary works created much controversy are the writers, Howard Phillips (H.P.) Lovecraft (1890-1937), Algernon Blackwood, (1869-1951) and Robert Ervin Howard, (1906-1936). Enigmatic characters like Rudolph Steiner (1861-1925) and Annie Besant (1847-1933) also flit back and forth like insects drawn to a mystical flame.

There were also a few who fall between the cracks of the categories covered above, like mainstream authors Ian Fleming (1908-1964) and Dennis Wheatley (1897-1977) and an antihero of the counter revolution, Charles Manson (1934-) plus his 'family'. Also there is the filmmaker and author, Kenneth Anger (1927-), and an associate of both Anger and Manson, Bobby Beausoleil (1947-), is also mentioned. Another unlikely source for such individuals is the US Army from whose ranks emerge the enigmatic Col John Alexander (1937-), Lt Col Michael Aquino (1946-) and others. It will quickly become evident that many of these names appear several times in relation to one another; this is because the majority of them were contemporaries who shared similar interests and motives.

Of the four self-styled magicians mentioned, two, Kenneth Grant and Osman Spare, dabbled extensively in Chaos Magic; on the other hand LaVey, also known as *'The Black Pope'*, was an avowed Satanist who founded his own church, *'The Church of Satan'*, and from his perspective his 'faith' was one of liberation rather than oppression and ultimately control. Crowley was slightly different again and followed a path of highly stylized ritual magic, sometimes called *'High Magic'* (or, as he had it, 'magick' and when discussing Crowley we shall use this spelling and the reason for this is explained later). Much of his magick was highly sexualized and incorporated elements of Tantrism, but was mainly based on ceremonies imitating the practices of *'The Hermetic Order of The Golden Dawn'* and the *'Ordo Templi Orientis'* or *'The Order of the Oriental Temple'*, sometimes simply referred to by the initials *'OTO'*. What none of them seemed to realize is that despite their individual claims to power, they all follow a common thread and that is the desire to alter realty to the whim and inclination of whomever operates the spell. The only method that makes any real sense is the sheer practicality of Chaos Magic as practiced by Grant and Spare, for it is on the precepts of Chaos Magic that all other magical theories and rites before and since are based. I have specifically used the spelling, 'magic', here because it does not apply to Crowley's interpretation.

Chapter 3
Chaos Magic

Before looking at some of the practitioners, let us briefly consider the premise upon which Chaos Magic and indeed all magic appears to work; given the length of this section of the book in comparison to the tomes and grimoires devoted to the subject, this may seem to be a rash statement, but once one examines the possible theory behind magic, irrespective of type, it all falls into place. The function of Chaos Theory on which the resultant magic is founded suggests that the more one wishes that something will happen the more likely it is that it will, in fact, occur. The most common illustration of this is so-called *'Butterfly Effect'*, a concept devised by the pioneer of chaos theory, Edward Lorenz, who suggested that the mere act of a butterfly or other small insect beating its wings in one location will create a tiny movement of air, which, through a series of events, is magnified and amplified until it becomes a hurricane thousands of miles away.

In Chaos Magic this is frequently summed up by the saying, *"Fake it till you make it"*, in other words, as an analogue of the butterfly flapping its wings, the tiny electrical force generated by one single thought, belief or desire can actually make it happen by changing the building blocks of reality. The actual process of Chaos Magic is produced through a type of intense meditation induced by the magician as he or she begins concentrating on the purpose of whatever spell they are creating. This can take the form of rhythmic body movements, dancing is the most common, in conjunction with hyperventilation to produce an altered state of consciousness. If there is an assistant present, at the moment when the magician seems on the point of collapse, the assistant should take hold of the magician from behind and put their arms around the solar plexus and squeeze.

The magician should by then have no thought in their mind other than the image of the spell, or the sigil of the spell, as a blinding white light filling every part of their being. On feeling themselves embraced by the assistant they should continue to hyperventilate and instantly release the spell from their mind allowing it to enter the quantum universe. It is at this point the helper should immediately release their hold, and assist the practitioner to fall to the floor, preferably onto cushions or similar. I cannot overstate the fact that this is a very risky procedure and could involve real damage to the magician; it is similar to a playground game where youngsters allow themselves to be rendered unconscious using the same method, the so-called 'game' is expressly forbidden by all schools.

The relevant words used here, and indeed all through this section of the book, for want of something better, are *'spell'*, *'magic'*, *'magick'*, *'sorcerer'*, *'wizard'*, *'mage'* and *'magician'*, but it does not really explain what is occurring and also carries with it considerable unnecessary negative baggage. What we see here once again is technology not mysticism; it is yet another example of the consequences of quantum physics in action. The best analogy for the arcane discipline of particle physics is as the mystical face of 'respectable' physics, in other words the world of quantum physics bears little resemblance to the conventions of Newtonian physics where everything has to obey specific laws. In the Newtonian world we inhabit, the universe itself is regarded as a machine that can be reduced down to its constituent parts, examined and reassembled.

There are immutable laws governing each and every facet of our world, such as cause and effect, action and reaction, all calculable and repeatable. The quantum world, as we have seen, is not predictable and can be influenced by such ephemeral forces as a single thought or emotion. The problem is that for the most part these infinitesimally small forces do not find expression at our level of existence and simply fizzle out. Examples of these subatomic forces are found in the oddity of quantum entanglement where two particles, e.g. photons, appear to exhibit the same reaction when a force is applied to one of them irrespective of how far apart they are. There are many examples of other, similar, phenomena taking place in the subatomic world that have no direct parallels in the Newtonian world and it is a situation that is deeply mistrusted by conventional science. If, as we have seen, quantum science is the mystical face of conventional science, then quantum physicists are a direct analogue of the magicians and necromancers of old and their equations and formulae equate to spells.

Oddly enough it is this very phenomenon of chaos in the world of computing that has encouraged the development of what are tentatively called *'chaotic circuits'* capable of changing their function in nanoseconds. In other words what starts out as, say, a processing unit, should it become necessary automatically changes its internal switching to perform a completely different function. These components are quite unique in that they are designed to be inherently chaotic unless instructed to take one form or another by an external control circuit to suit the needs of any particular situation. It is also predicted that components such as these will have a capability for self-repair.

While this is obviously a very simplified account of what is currently in development it nevertheless allows a glimpse into the bizarre world of quantum science where, right now, scientists are attempting to bond DNA chemistry with quantum mechanics to edge ever closer to a viable quantum computer and the development of a such a device will, literally, take our search for knowledge to the next level. A very small and mundane experiment to demonstrate Chaos Magic can be attempted by simply setting out on a shopping trip by car with the certainty that there will be a convenient parking place available when you get there, 99 times out of 100 there will be. Do not dismiss this as sheer luck for it is not; it is very simple to test and carry out, and it is exactly what Chaos Magic is about. One word of caution, before carrying out this simple experiment you have to absolutely believe 100% that it will work; there must be no room in your mind for any doubt.

Chapter 4
The Magicians

Aleister Edward Crowley (1875-1947)

Do what thou will shall be the whole of the law, love is the law, love under will.

I have chosen to begin with Aleister Crowley, because he, through his sheer notoriety and chutzpah, has carved himself a lasting niche in the psyche of the general public, and particularly within the ranks of the so-called New Age movement. Although he died in 1947, there is no doubt that he still influences the practices of the vast majority of the magickal and quasi-magickal groups that have been created since. Anyone who doubts this has only to enter one of the many shops trading in the implements and substances used in mystical rituals and there will almost certainly be a selection of his books, which are still in print, and sets of the Thoth Tarot cards designed by Crowley and painted by Lady Frieda Harris. This tarot deck was not printed in the lifetime of either Crowley or Lady Harris, but in 1969 one of his legion of fans had it published, it has since been reprinted twice, 1977 and 1986.

That Aleister Edward Crowley regarded himself as special is without question and he demonstrated this by a display of total indifference to the fact that he was branded alternately as, the *'Wickedest Man in the World'* and the *'Great Beast 666'*, both titles awarded by the British media that gave him immense and abiding satisfaction and doubtless encouraged him to greater excesses. In addition to his magickal aspirations, Crowley aspired to a louche, hedonistic and largely degenerate lifestyle and following his university education frittered away much of his inheritance of £30,000 (approx. $55,000) on pleasure and the pursuit of magical power as he saw it. This sum was left to him in 1895 and in today's terms was probably worth in the region of £500,000 (or approx. $890,000). He was also a mountaineer of some note, although when the going got really tough he always made sure his survival was paramount, to the point of abandoning his fellow mountaineers to their fate during one unfortunate expedition.

That aside, his lifestyle provoked revulsion and outrage in the late Victorian society in which he lived, particularly his many indiscrete sexual encounters with both sexes. There was no doubt that he was charismatic and attracted several wealthy followers and patrons who were necessary to fund his exploits after his own money eventually ran out. It is curious that his generous inheritance had come from his father's interests in a brewing business, particularly as his father and to a greater extent his mother were both strict Plymouth Brethren, a still existing evangelical Christian protestant schism that takes a stern view of anything that might be pleasurable. It was actually his mother, a particularly blinkered member of the sect, who decided that all was not well with her son and it was from her that the young Crowley first heard himself addressed as *'The Beast of Revelation'*.

Incidentally, why his parents joyless take on scripture did not include the production and sale of alcohol is far from clear, but as is frequently the way with those who apparently follow strict biblical protocols, hypocrisy is almost a prerequisite. Most of those that do disapprove of alcohol tend to forget that their Messiah allegedly changed water into wine, his first miracle (or magical display depending on how one views him), while a guest at the wedding feast at Canaan. Nowadays this event is usually looked upon as an allegory and there is some disputed evidence that the wedding feast was actually his own. As regards Crowley's upbringing, one thing that is also known is that as a child he was forced to maintain a lifestyle that adopted the codes of the Plymouth Brethren, who believe in the literal truth of scripture, and as a result caused him to state later in his life that he had both a thorough knowledge of The Bible and an equal abhorrence of it.

Be that as it may, when Crowley eventually did emerge from university he soon embraced the path of dissolution with considerable enthusiasm, which quickly developed into a fascination and obsession with magick and the magickal arts. The first steps in his journey came in the form a book on black magick written by a member of *'The Hermetic Order of the Golden Dawn'*. His choice of the term, 'magick', seems to be based on his perception that the alternative spelling, 'magic', referred to sleight of hand and stage illusions, and his intention was the use of the genuine article – it is an interpretation shared by various magicians. The revelations in the book did not entirely suit him as he wanted something much darker with more 'meat' attached to it, but it sufficiently whetted his appetite for further investigation. At around this time he became a member of the *'Celtic Church'*, an organization that was rather ethereal in outlook and operated in an atmosphere of fairies, wizards and certain magical rites which was of course not what he desired, but at the time better that nothing. Unsurprisingly he was also claimed to be a member of the Freemasons and the Rosicrucians, although the membership protocols of Freemasonry should have automatically excluded him.

While continuing his search he read whatever books on magick and alchemy he could lay his hands on. As a result of this he met a genuine alchemist, Julian Baker, a chemist by profession, who, after becoming convinced of Crowley's desire to learn more, introduced him to a colleague. Baker's colleague in turn introduced him to Samuel Liddel (MacGregor) Mathers, the leader, founder and high priest of *'The Golden Dawn'*; at last, although he did not at first realize it, Crowley was on course. Initially at least Mathers and Crowley struck up a friendship: both were well educated, both were snobs, both were dreamers and both were fascinated by the possibilities that magick might hold. At around this point Crowley actually became a member of The Golden Dawn and found its rituals and theatrics much more to his taste, and shortly after this he purchased Boleskine House on the shores of Loch Ness in Scotland. As it transpired some time later Crowley came to be called, *'The other Loch Ness monster'*.

An example of Mathers strong fantasy streak was typified when he began to award himself the rank of Count (or 'Compte' as he preferred it, his wife quite naturally adopting the title of 'Comptesse'). He also adopted the name MacGregor and incorporated this into other fictitious titles, *'MacGregor of Glenstrae'*, and *'Count of Glenstrae'*. Crowley also had a desire for the trappings of rank and at one point during a short term with the British diplomatic service adopted the name, *'Count Vladimir Svareff'*, complete with *faux* Russian accent. It is interesting that many notables in the murky world of the esoteric and mystical arts evidently have a need and desire to adopt generally undeserved titles and doctorates.

Although this is typical on the man, it is fair to assume that these ego-boosting additions might help their standing in the circles in which they operate and add a measure of veracity to both their position and views. After his initiation into Mathers' Golden Dawn, where he was given the secret name of *'Frater Perdurabo'*, (literally, 'enduring brother'), Crowley took a flat in Chancery Lane, London. Here he set aside two rooms to serve as temples for the practice his alternative 'religion', which by now was entirely 'magickal' in nature. Many people still ask whether he was a 'black' or 'white' magician with no real appreciation of what this means other than the poorly understood emotional baggage carried by these two adjectives, but it is still a fair point and the answer appears to be relatively straightforward.

If one can accept the fundamental premise that the driving force behind magick is something real, and we have already looked at a simple test to demonstrate this, then the reality becomes apparent. From my own perspective there is no such thing as 'black or 'white' magick, there are only the techniques that lie behind the practice and operation of that esoteric and ephemeral branch of science and technology. The problems begin with the purpose for which that technology is used, for it is whoever creates and operates the technology that decides and directs its ultimate outcome. An analogy for this lies in the use or abuse of medicine; in other words medicines can be used to both heal or to kill. As with the power behind magic on its own, it represents a potential for both 'good' and 'evil', but its application depends on the inclination of whoever uses it. Crowley appears to have drawn his inspiration and probably much of his power from nature rather than some notional trans-dimensional entity like Satan or 'The Devil' and this is something that is not generally appreciated.

There is no doubt whatsoever that he was dedicated, totally, to becoming an accomplished magician, and to this end he began studying and practicing the magick of '*Abramelin the Mage*', a virtually forgotten practitioner of spells and incantations, references to whom had previously been unearthed by Mathers in the records of The Bibleotheque Nationale in Paris. We should not underestimate the scholarship of Mathers who was no bored dilettante; although he was very serious about his choice of hobby he was also rather more interested in the assumed 'glamour' of the 'differentness' associated with magick rather than in its lifestyle and philosophy. Crowley had willing assistance in his endeavors from his then flat mate and fellow member of The Golden Dawn, Allan Bennett. Their adherence to the rituals developed by the magician, Abramelin, was later to feature in a six month long ritual performed by Crowley at Boleskine House in what is perhaps his Magnum Opus. It might be argued that his abilities continued to increase after this event, but when viewed dispassionately, rather than improve his talents he began a long, slow, spiral into degeneracy and addiction with no obvious contribution to the canon of magickal lore, at least that is, until the last few years of his hugely eventful life, but we will return to this a little later.

Boleskine House, which is on the south east shore of the loch and stands in 47 acres of ground, was built as a hunting lodge in the late 19th century and was owned by Crowley from 1899 until 1913. It was for some time regarded as the very centre of Thelemic power, and because of its isolated location it was deliberately chosen by him to perform The Abramelin Ritual. This ceremony, rather than relying on the traditional accoutrements of pentagrams and the invocation of demons, is almost peaceful and mystical by comparison. The working involves almost continual prayer over a period of six months at a 'Holy Place' set aside for the purpose. If the ceremony, which along with its outcome we will look at shortly, is successful, the materialization of the magician's guardian angel occurs. Thelemic magick as defined by its creator, is *'The science and art of causing change in conformity with will'*, and is a distillation created by him, which encompasses techniques drawn from Yoga, the Cabala, the Tarot, astrology and a series of powerful invocations. Remarkably, this is precisely what lies at the very core of Chaos magick and the failure to recognize the fact is perhaps more to do with the ego of the practitioner rather than any shortcomings in the techniques.

It is worth noting that Boleskine House still stands and since Crowley's departure has been the dwelling place of several families with no apparent interest in either Magick or Crowley. In fact its previous occupier has proved something of an embarrassment and various tenants since still have to put up with the unwanted attentions of the merely curious and others who have a vested interest its murky past. Its most famous owner was the musician, Jimmy Page, the lead guitarist with the iconic rock band Led Zeppelin and well-known 'Crowleyfile', and although owning it for several years he seldom actually stayed there. It has occasionally been alleged that Page did attempt some of Crowley's rituals and that his interest in magick went beyond mere scholarship, but this has never been confirmed and certainly not by Page himself.

During his tenure, one of Page's friends lived there with his family, taking care of the fabric of the building and generally looking after the place. While he was in residence both he and his young family allegedly had a few unsettling encounters within the grounds and the house itself. Jimmy Page also moved in other magical circles and at one stage was involved with the notorious film director and disciple of Aleister Crowley, Kenneth Anger, and agreed to write the musical score for one of Angers' films depicting magic rituals and entitled *'Lucifer Rising'*. Evidently the film director was not too enamored with what Page had composed and they fell out with Anger promising to throw a curse on both Page and by association the entire band. As we will see, this era during the 1960's produced an entire sub-culture that seemed to revolve around the twin subjects of hedonism, magick and drugs. The results of this unhealthy combination were quite predictable.

The fall out occurred in 1977, when the guitarist had in fact bodily ejected the film director from his basement flat, and although Jimmy appeared to shrug off the incident, others regard what happened as pivotal in the demise of Led Zeppelin. Following on from what occurred, in 1977, Karac, the infant son of Zeppelin singer Robert Plant, died from an infection and in September 1980 the band's drummer, John Bonham, died after an extended drinking session. This seems to have been the last straw and in December the same year the band broke up although both Page and Plant still work together on various projects. This included a special one-off reunion concert in 2008, which was an immediate sell out. Whether or not the tragedies were the direct result of Anger's curse is a moot point, e.g. Bonham was noted for his drinking habits and children do get sick and sadly sometimes die; nevertheless the curse was made and these deaths ensued. Even the end of Led Zeppelin as a band did not silence the rumors, which continued to suggest that the entire band with the exception of Bonham had signed a deal with Satan to ensure their earthly success. While probably baseless, these rumors persisted for some time and were almost certainly founded on the association between Page and his fascination with Crowley's works.

There is no real evidence that the Abramelin Ritual was entirely successful, but it is known that while it was in progress there was constant darkness in the house even during the daytime necessitating keeping the lights on. This was accompanied by a series of events involving the housekeeper, the local butcher and a tradesman who attempted to kill Crowley. There were further issues when he was forced to abandon the ritual for some weeks while he traveled to Paris to help deal with some problems affecting the internal politics of The Golden Dawn. It is claimed that he failed to take proper precautions while temporarily closing the ritual and some of the entities brought forth by Crowley were not sent back (or adequately contained) and escaped to wander the hills and woodland surrounding the loch. He did eventually return and complete the ritual, but it may not have had the intended outcome due to the untimely interruption. Crowley went on to become head of The Golden Dawn in both Britain and Europe, but due to his ego and almost instinctive desire for change this did not last and he was expelled. Undaunted he went on the join the OTO, who, knowing his reputation, should perhaps have known better. Incidentally, while not in the manner envisaged by its founder, Thelema is still practiced and Boleskine House is, for good or ill, still regarded as its spiritual centre, rather as The Vatican is viewed as the heart of the Catholic Church and Mecca that of Islam.

Crowley and a small entourage eventually decamped to Sicily where they founded the *'Abbey of Thelema'* in Sicily. This was not actually a building with any former religious heritage, rather it was an isolated stone built villa, well off the beaten track, something that once again was ideally suited to his purposes. The excesses conducted at the 'abbey' eventually came to the ears of the then Italian dictator, Benito Mussolini and led to the eventual expulsion of Crowley and his followers from Sicily. Nevertheless, the siren call of magick still wove its spell and Crowley continued to refine and develop the rituals of the OTO, especially the sexual Tantric element and as was his talent, succeeded in upsetting many of the members.

Tantrism is a mystical offshoot of Hinduism based on the precept that if you can achieve union with the universe the gateway to true spirituality can be achieved. Once again it becomes obvious that the ancient dictum of 'all is one' is an absolute, irrespective of how one cares to dress it up in new clothes. In fact the plethora of cults and schisms that espouse new revelations and insights may indicate a case of 'The emperor's new spirituality' than any genuine breakthrough in understanding. On a more personal level it tends to bring focus to the premise that we are part of the universe and the universe is part of us. Crowley's continuing fascination with mysticism and magick eventually led to the formation of the *'Argenteum Astrum'* or *'Order of The Silver Star'*, sometimes referred to simply as the A\A\, a self-devised and ritual laden organization born out his membership of the OTO, although the A\A\appears to have been more introspective and mystically inclined rather than in any sense Satanic.

At around this time he befriended and embarked on a homosexual dalliance with another occultist, Victor Neuberg, who assisted him in his efforts, which included the extremely risky invocation of a demon; but even Crowley drew the line when Neuberg suggested that they abduct, rape, murder and dismember a young woman and offer her remains to Thoth. This, however, did not prevent him from carrying on much as before, presumably with varying degrees of success. The suggestion of the need for blood sacrifice is one of the more lurid and repugnant aspects of the pursuit of Magick and reflects the belief that human, or indeed animal, blood carries the promise of power. This stems from the assumption that whatever entity is being invoked requires the presence of fresh blood to give it substance and 'take on flesh'. Again there is some disagreement here because some schools of thought insist that it is the release of 'life energy' at the point of death that provides the motive power rather than the blood itself and therefore the sacrifice of a living creature is the most potent method. We will return to the possible association between blood sacrifice and the spiritualist phenomenon of *'ectoplasm'* a little later in this account.

As Crowley ploughed on with his quest he went to Egypt where, after some discrete enquiries or perhaps simple bribery, – something that at the time was common among those charged with guarding Egyptian antiquities – he obtained permission from the Egyptian authorities to meditate overnight in the Kings Chamber of the great Pyramid. According to Crowley's biography this was a remarkable experience. He and his wife entered the chamber at dusk and settled themselves down. When Crowley extinguished the lights and he and his wife began meditating, a blue light emanated from the walls allowing him to read from certain works dedicated to Thoth that he had brought with him. This unusual form of illumination lasted for the entire night, only fading when the dawn came.

Alas, Crowley's lifestyle and his addictions, including one for heroin, eventually took their toll on both his already stretched finances and his health; after a time in America he returned to Britain during the late 1930's, but things had changed and the world was, once again, almost at war and there was quite enough wickedness around without any 'magickal' assistance. His attempts to shock and outrage society became much more muted, and he ended his days destitute and addicted in a nursing home where, on the 1st December 1947 at the age of 72, he died and we shall return to the significant number 72 a little later.

However, it was during his final days in America that he became friendly with two other up-and-coming magicians, Jack Parsons and L. Ron Hubbard. Parsons was one of the founders of the Jet Propulsion Laboratory (JPL) in Pasadena, California, and Hubbard achieved fame, or perhaps notoriety, as the founder of *'The Church of Scientology'*. They are known to have consulted Crowley concerning one ritual they attempted, the so called *'Amalantrah Working'*, which evidently failed to achieve the desired result, but the later *'Babalon Working'* (sic) carried out in 1947 was an attempt to open a fissure in space-time to either allow the creation of an artificial being called a *'Homunculus'*, or bring one into this universe. Incidentally, while Hubbard died of natural causes, Parsons did not. His demise was apparently due, not to magickal dabbling, but through a desire to bring his work home with him. His job with the JPL involved experimenting with various rocket propellants and evidently he was doing this at home in his garage when the volatile chemicals exploded thereby ending his life. Incidentally the Church of Scientology is quick to point out that its founder was only involved with Parsons (and magick) in order to monitor him in case he divulged any military secrets to a foreign power. No doubt they are correct.

Whether or not the Babalon Working was effective is, as with other rituals, not obvious, but one curious fact is that since 1947 there have been a rapid succession of odd and anomalous sightings, particularly of UFO related phenomena in a range of places and situations. It is also known that Parsons developed a liking for Crowley, and this was apparently reciprocated to the point that Crowley often referred to Parsons as 'his son'. Following his death and his cremation in Brighton he still achieved a measure of notoriety: his eulogy, the self-penned '*Hymn to Pan*', was read to the assembled congregation. Brighton council was duly shocked and outraged, vowing that never again would such a thing be permitted on its premises. This was a fairly easy promise to make since it is not likely that a man such as Aleister Crowley would ever be seen again. It is probably an example of changing values, but magick aside, his exploits and excesses are no more outrageous and perhaps even less so than those of many modern rock stars and others of the super-rich whose lifestyles are less than savory. In fact, had Crowley existed now is it is entirely possible that he would have been feted and encouraged in his efforts by an army of fans and disciples; he might even have been a messiah.

Chapter 5
Ectoplasm

The earlier mention of the alleged use of blood sacrifice brings us to another related matter: belief in the efficacy of blood is reflected in the much later phenomenon of enigmatic substances like *'ectoplasm'* manifested during mediumistic séances where the presence of this substance apparently allows the 'spirit entity' to take shape. The ectoplasm, which is supposedly biological in nature, exuded directly from the bodily orifices of the medium and allowed the spirit to materialize, or, as we have seen, *'take on flesh'*, which seems to be in a direct parallel with the invocation of more overtly malign entities. There is still much controversy about whether or not ectoplasm is a genuine phenomenon, because most of the contemporary photographs taken of mediums producing it are the most naïve and obvious fakes; nevertheless there may be some truth in it. The word, ectoplasm, the name of which derived from the Greek, *'ektos'*, or 'outside', was first adopted by the French physiologist, Charles Richet, and its original context applied only to the *'cytoplasm'* found on the exterior of a human cell wall.

Researchers who claim to have studied actual samples of the substance describe it as cold to the touch and rubbery in texture, while other insist that it is much more fluid, slimy and like gauze in nature. It is also claimed that when it first appears from the body of the medium it is very fragile, but eventually hardens and solidifies. In one experiment conducted in the very early 20th century, a medium named Kathleen Goligher produced a kind of ectoplasm that was strong enough to register on a set of scales (corresponding weight loss in mediums producing the substance has also been recorded) and was able to lift small tables and other items. In an article written by Professor Susan Blackmore, the female medium involved was reportedly supplied with clothing by the test team prior to the experiment and a special dye was used to trace the course of the ectoplasm as it withdrew into her body.

Unfortunately much better evidence is sadly lacking since ectoplasm will not appear in the presence of light – in fact 'spirit' in general is generally not well disposed to lighting either. There are many reasons proffered for this unfortunate set of circumstances; they may even be correct too, since it is also claimed that 'spirit' exists at a different frequency from the physical world and the frequency that white light produces (white light of course combines all visible frequencies of light) may actively interfere with it. However, since infrared photography precludes the necessity for conventional light sources it would be ideal for the purpose, but this too has proven less than successful. One of the few pieces of ectoplasm still in existence is held by the London based Society for Psychical Research (SPR) and resembles a large section of fine muslin; curiously enough it is also neatly seamed at the edges.

Other small pieces of the substance obtained during séances have proved to consist of decidedly non-paranormal substances including chiffon and fragments of skin. The only medium at the time of writing claiming to produce ectoplasm is David Thompson; the difference here is that he is prepared to do so under infrared lighting. Just why the number of physical mediums with the ability to exude this substance has fallen so dramatically in the last 60 years is unknown. But sadly, as with any field that satisfies the needs and frailty of human beings, there are always those who will exploit it in any way they can, usually for financial reasons. We must remember that while this does not preclude the genuineness of ectoplasm as a vehicle for visitors from the astral world we should also be aware that fakes and frauds are out there too.

Chapter 6
The Magician and The Spooks

One of the most curious aspects of Crowley's life is also the one about which the least is known, although much speculated about; and that is his relationship with the authors Ian Fleming and Dennis Wheatley and it is one that is well worth exploring. Ian Lancaster Fleming is obviously best known for his literary creation, the fictional superspy James Bond, but in this instance it is his non-literary occupations that are of most interest to us. Born to a wealthy family in 1908 in the expensive Mayfair area of London, his father, Valentine Fleming, was a member of parliament and there can be little doubt that the subtle aura of power and influence was something to which he became accustomed almost by a form of osmosis. His mother was named Evelyn St Croix Rose and the very nature of her surname should pique the interest of those with even a slight knowledge of the esoteric and arcane, although whether this is an example of some strange synchronicity or sheer blind luck is debatable. Remember one thing though, when dealing with this subject very little happens by chance, particularly when it includes anything involving The Great Beast.

St Croix Rose, the rose cross: might this be a reference to the 'rosy cross' of the Rosicrucians, or, since the rose is also a symbol of secrecy, might it also have been a precursor of the murky world that her son went on to inhabit in the Naval Intelligence Service? Might it even have some lineal connection with that mysterious order of warrior monks, The Knights Templar, who wore the red Croix Pattee, literally a 'rosy cross' upon their mantles? Although Ian Fleming had no obvious religious affiliations with any particular belief or schism, he did lead a particularly active, successful and secretive career during the Second World War. However, yet another odd circumstance emerges when one discovers that one of his cousins is none other than the actor Christopher Lee, someone who established his reputation playing the part of Abraham (Bram) Stokers creation, the ultimate vampire Count Dracula. Incidentally, Stoker was also allegedly involved in occult groups such as *'The Hermetic Order of The Golden Dawn'*; might this be a further tantalizing example of the coinciding orbits of those with the same interests?

The association with Dracula, (and for that matter the Frankenstein monster), is something that Lee does not particularly relish, but nonetheless it is with these roles that he is most often associated. His distinctive cavernous features, and perhaps also his reputation, lead to him being cast as the dark wizard Saruman in Peter Jackson's wonderful film adaptation of Tolkein's epic trilogy of books collectively known as 'The Lord of the Rings'. As we shall see, he also played another part that was closely associated with the black arts, that of the Duc de Richelieu in the film version of Dennis Wheatley's *'The Devil Rides Out'*; it is also one more synchronicity linking Fleming and Wheatley, but more of this later. Again one gets the feeling that it's like small pieces in a puzzle remorselessly falling into place – like attracting like even in the ephemeral world of the cinema. This strange sense of inevitability and fate occurs regularly in almost all aspects of life; it is frequently noticed by authors when seeking out some obscure element (or indeed inspiration) relating to whatever subject or story they happen to be researching, that it finds the seeker rather than the other way round. It has occurred to this author many times, so often in fact that when it occurs I now smile ruefully and murmur my thanks and appreciation to whatever agency supplies it.

While a subaltern in the Scottish Black Watch regiment, in

1939 with the start of World War II Fleming was quickly seconded into Naval Intelligence by none other than its director, Vice Admiral John Godfrey, where he initially served as his personal assistant. His first naval commission was as a lieutenant in the Royal Navy Volunteer Reserve, but he was soon promoted, first to Lieutenant Commander then to a full Commander. This is of course the same rank as his creation, James Bond, although Fleming's code number, unlike Bond's 007, was 17F. The 007 designation does have occult connections though, it was the code name used by Dr John Dee, the medieval magician, astrologer, alchemist and advisor to Queen Elizabeth 1st, when he helped found the British Secret Service with Sir Francis Walsingham. In the early stages of WWII it is claimed that Fleming had the idea of luring Rudolph Hess, then Adolph Hitler's trusted deputy, to Britain in an attempt to contact a supposedly fictitious clandestine group of highly placed and influential anti-Churchill Englishmen. The plan involved using the influence of Aleister Crowley to plant the required disinformation via his long established links with Karl Theodor Reuss the head of the OTO.

Crowley first became involved with Reuss in 1910, and Reuss's pedigree suited Crowley admirably: in addition to the OTO, he was also a high ranking Freemason, a Rosicrucian and a member of the Illuminati, although with this supposed organization it is difficult to decide which version of it this might have been. Reuss's own background was likewise connected with the security and intelligence services in Germany starting in the 1880's with the Prussian secret police. It was on their behalf that he visited London at the very beginning of the 20th century to join the *'Socialist League'*, a radical left wing organization headed by the daughter of the political philosopher and revolutionary Karl Marx, who along with Lenin, Trotsky and Engels was renowned as one of the main protagonists of the Russian Revolution.

It is fair to comment that this popular revolt had created ripples of disquiet and unease in the Royal Houses throughout

Europe and beyond, and there was very real fear that the House of Windsor might be next. Given the class ridden and divided society existing in Britain at the time it was a threat that had to be taken very seriously. It was also the beginning of the still ongoing process of taking various weapons out of civilian ownership and making their legal possession an exceedingly laborious process. It had, predictably, little or no effect on the illegal possession of firearms, but it was never intended to. By a coincidence the link between Marx and London is still intact; his body currently lies in the grounds of London's Highgate Cemetery. Reuss was eventually exposed and after leaving Britain he continued to work for German Intelligence in the Balkans and the Middle East.

According to the author, researcher and consultant for Washington DC's Spy Museum, Richard Spence, Crowley's involvement with spying goes back to his time at Cambridge University where he was member of a right-wing group called *'The Primrose League'* that supposedly spied on anyone who did not wholeheartedly support the policies of the ruling Conservative Party. It is not uncommon for groups like this to exist and proliferate in universities, which are popular hunting grounds for intelligence agencies of all persuasions, for the young are nothing if not passionate about whatever cause they choose to embrace. Perhaps more importantly they frequently lack the experience and discrimination to make informed choices, something that is easily and eagerly exploited by prospective political 'handlers' who will radicalize them and tell them exactly what they want to hear.

For his part, just prior to the First World War having now become a member of the OTO – he was in fact initiated by none other than Reuss himself – Crowley allegedly used his connections with his mentor to spy on the activities of the German government. When the war did break out in 1914 Crowley was living in the United States and according to the British press he used his time to write seditious pamphlets and articles decrying the British Empire and all it stood for. He later claimed that he only did this to throw his enemies off the track by spreading disinformation, and, in addition, was acting on behalf of the British Secret Service. Typically, given the aversion for transparency in the United Kingdom, both then and even more so now, this is something that they categorically denied, but it now appears that there may have been more than an element of truth in his claims.

It was very easy to make mud stick to Crowley – he was already excoriated on every possible occasion by the popular press, so to paint him as both traitor and turncoat as well was a simple job. However, it now seems probable that he really was working at spreading 'black' propaganda on behalf of the British Secret Intelligence Service (SIS now better known as MI6) and probably the Naval Intelligence Department (NID) too, by infiltrating pro-German organizations under the guise of a rabid Irish republican hell-bent on acting against the interests of the United Kingdom. In truth it is difficult to see how he achieved this because his accent was decidedly upper class English, but perhaps the Americans with whom he associated would not realize this.

Having said that, as we have already seen, he had already successfully passed himself off as a minor Russian aristocrat so he may also have possessed a gift for mimicry. With this background it should come as no surprise that, assuming his network of contacts was still intact, he might be interested in working on some clandestine missions for the intelligence community once again. This was exactly what Ian Fleming suggested to his head of department in relation to the proposed plot to ensnare Rudolph Hess, but there are at least three alternative sets of opinion on what actually occurred. One clearly states that Crowley was never approached for the simple reason that Hess flew to Britain apparently of his own volition to broker a secret peace deal through the aegis of the Duke of Hamilton, which rendered the plan obsolete.

Another opinion suggests that although Hess did in fact parachute from his Messerschmitt Me110 fighter aircraft into a farmer's field near Eaglesham, which is close to the city of Glasgow in Scotland, his arrest and subsequent lengthy interrogation revealed some interesting possibilities. Before continuing it should be made clear that when Hess was first arrested he announced to his captors in almost unaccented English that he was 'Captain Alfred Horn' and for, at the time unspecified reasons, asked to be taken directly to the Duke of Hamilton. The location where Hess actually landed was apparently not just a random selection either, but was in fact part of the vast estate belonging to the previously mentioned Duke of Hamilton.

Following his arrest and subsequent intensive questioning, along with much needed strategic and political information, his interrogators regarded some of what he said as extremely obscure and possibly occult in nature. Fortunately, because Fleming was personally involved in the interrogations, he suggested that Crowley be drafted in to help make sense of what was being said. He also had the idea that if a belief in the occult was something that was prevalent among the German high command, then it might be successfully used as a weapon against them. It was at this point that Maxwell Knight, the deputy head of MI6, refused to have any part of the scheme and for reasons best known to himself absolutely forbade any meeting between Crowley and Hess. This decision caused a heated argument, but Knight apparently emerged victorious and the meeting never took place, although Crowley did in fact write to Fleming who was by now the director of Naval Intelligence with an offer of help, which was apparently rejected.

This is quite at odds with a third account according to Richard Spence in his book, *'Secret Agent 666'*. Crowley was very friendly with Maxwell Knight and through him had been introduced to both Commander Ian Fleming and Dennis Wheatley, who was also involved in the security services as part of Winston Churchill's highly secret 'Planning Committee for Total Warfare'. The account given by Spence suggests that Hess's flight to Britain was not a spontaneous decision, but was the successful result of a joint disinformation operation by MI5 and Naval Intelligence. He further claims that Crowley did interview Hess at an interrogation centre in south London and not just once either, which provided a wealth of background information on the opinions held by some of the German military and civilian hierarchy. One of these influences was a belief in the efficacy of Astrology, which led to a series of bogus astrological charts being created with the objective of misdirecting those who were prepared to use them as templates for their decisions. One other factor was the use of British astrologers to cast charts for specific times and dates on the assumption that the German astrologers would be producing similar information for their masters. This, it was thought, would allow a measure of foreknowledge of how they might react, whether this did actually produce any viable results is not recorded.

If Crowley did actually meet Hess it obviously infers that Knight either approved of the meeting or at least acquiesced to it. Spence quotes the difficulty he experienced in obtaining information from MI5 and MI6 regarding Crowley's role with both organizations, both flatly denying any knowledge of his involvement with them. This is to be expected when dealing with these organizations and is an entirely appropriate and instinctive reaction on their part. Following the initial denials from MI5, Spence found a reference to Crowley dating from the 1930's in the Public Records Office in London and he returned to MI5 with this information. The agency were most apologetic and admitted that they did have a file on him at one point, but it had been 'destroyed' at some time during the 1950's.

The whole issue of Hess and his subsequent imprisonment in

Spandau prison is in many ways as intriguing and mysterious as the accusations of occult practices laid against him. The issues are mostly 'whys'? Why for example did Hess just happen to 'steal' an aircraft from the Messerschmitt factory that had just been fitted with larger fuel tanks at his specific request? Why was the aircraft allowed to get as far inland as Eaglesham with no sign of either land based anti-aircraft fire or intercepting RAF fighters? Why did he really want to see the Duke of Hamilton in the first place? Following his death in 1987 at the age of 93, supposedly through suicide, why were the documents relating to the case locked away as state secrets for 65 years?

Actually this is no real surprise when one considers the UK Government's abysmal record of concealment and denial, but it leaves us with many questions and few answers. However it is known that in Great Britain there was a highly placed and influential pacifist leaning lobby that included the Duke of Hamilton who was a serving RAF Wing Commander. In fact there was also a measure of pro-Nazi/German sentiment prevalent in the highest offices, elected and otherwise, in the land. This appears to give credence to the hypothesis that Hess intended to negotiate a peace treaty through those with whom Hamilton was associated. Whether Hamilton's associates were those 'anti-Churchill' figures referred to earlier is a moot point, but it is likely that they were. As history shows, this meeting did not happen, therefore we can only speculate on the outcome if it had.

Shortly after this Spence unearthed more information concerning another MI5 file on Crowley dating from 1943, and when he once again approached them with this he found to his surprise that this too had been 'destroyed'. There was also apparently a Scotland Yard file on Crowley and, in addition, there were three additional files on his activities from 1906 until 1916 secreted away in the British Foreign Office. This is of course fascinating, but since Spence could not access these files we must only guess at their contents; and, although they might well confirm his work on behalf of the intelligence services, equally they might provide evidence Crowley, due to his connections overseas, was under the surveillance of the secret services in case he was acting as an enemy agent.

Having said that I can fully sympathies with Mr Spence because I had the same run-around, although not from the British intelligence community; in this instance I was awarded near identical treatment from the US Army Intelligence Dept at Ft. George G. Meade in Maryland, USA. I had requested information on a phenomenon called 'The Hutchison Effect' (HE) under the US Freedom of Information Act (FOIA) from Ft Meade regarding a series of scientific evaluations they carried out on electromagnetics researcher John Hutchison's discoveries at his lab located in Vancouver, Canada. They flatly denied that these evaluations had ever taken place until I provided copies of documents relating to the case that had originated from their offices; these they immediately informed me were obvious forgeries.

I then supplied more documentation from the same source and asked if these too were fakes; at this point I was referred to the Los Alamos National Laboratory (LANL) in Albuquerque in New Mexico. After a short correspondence, the LANL remembered the case and provided some points of contact, but were unable to supply any copies of any files, because they had unfortunately 'lost' them. They helpfully indicated that there was no point in contacting Ft Meade again because they also had 'lost' their copies of the files. Evidently, depending on what is required, the Freedom of Information Act in both the UK and the USA is not especially helpful. One thing that did become evident was that according to the small amount of new information that did emerge from the LANL, one common factor linking 'The Hutchison Effect' with many other borderline scientific 'black projects' was one name, Colonel John Alexander. Although obviously from a later era and not ostensibly connected with magic (or even magick), Col Alexander assumes an almost

Crowley-like link connecting many apparently diverse subjects and people. The one thing the projects and subjects he features in all have in common is that they border on the anomalous and unusual whether they be military or in his personal interests, and sometime it is nigh on impossible to tell the difference; we shall return to Col Alexander in Chapter 7.

Chapter 7
Dennis Wheatley

Dennis Wheatley for his part is renowned as a writer of occult fiction involving Satanism, devil worship and black magic. The other factor that really binds these men together is their involvement with, once again, the magus in chief, Aleister Crowley. Although as we have seen there may have been some interest by the British security services regarding his activities, and he may or may not have acted on behalf of British interests as a spy, that was not his fascination for Wheatley. The author already had a deep and abiding interest in the occult and the paranormal, but when researching his book, *The Devil Rides Out,* he sought an introduction to Crowley through the good graces of the homosexual politician Tom Driberg. To his surprise they got on well and became very friendly, and to make sure that all bases were covered he also consulted Montague Summers, a noted expert on witchcraft and a self-styled Catholic priest. Wheatley also took Crowley's earlier book, *The Moonchild,* as source material for his own, and unlike the source his own book became extremely successful.

For all his growing success as a writer, Wheatley had some serious character flaws, which found expression in his right-wing views and his absolute distaste for any kind of social equality (let alone socialism), and in his novel, *Contraband,* he wrote 'Communism is the new face of Satanism'. This jingoistic nationalism (which by the standards of today is almost humorous) – with its many references to 'Johnny foreigner', and 'untrustworthy foreigners' – was also expressed in his fervent desire to maintain the 'old order' where the ruling classes ruled and the underclass's knew their place with much deference to their masters. In many ways Wheatley was a living embodiment of the archetypal 'little Englander' and his secondment to Churchill's planning staff was much to his liking since it gave him ample opportunity to express his views at what he considered an appropriate level.

Following the war, in 1953 he produced another best-selling occult novel, *To The Devil a Daughter,* which in 1976 was made into a film of the same name directed by Peter Sykes, and once again featuring Christopher Lee in one of the leading roles; in 1960 came another novel, *The Satanist.* One thing that, in my opinion, Wheatley did have right was his view of magic and how it operates; it also is heavily redolent of Crowley's ideas. Through one of his characters, the Duc de Richlieu, as played by Christopher Lee, he cautions that, *'In magic there is neither good nor evil, it is merely a science. The science of causing change to occur by means of one's will, the sinister reputation attached to it is entirely groundless and based on superstition rather than objective observation. The power of the will is something that people do not understand, attributing to it mysterious qualities that it does not possess'*. It could even be the old magician himself talking.

Chapter 8
The Benevolent Spook

Col John Alexander

Although something of an outsider when one considers the type of characters described thus far, the previously mentioned Col John Alexander deserves closer attention because this man has had a hand in several ideas, concepts, experiments and plots that in any other context might be described as magical. Although retired for many years, he was, and perhaps still is, one of the few who really understands the Machiavellian world of plots and counterplots, rumors and disinformation that blight the murky world of the intelligence services. This is not to say that Col Alexander was a chair jockey who ran his shadowy empire from an office; far from it, Alexander was someone who was quite prepared to get his hands dirty should the need arise. By this I do not mean that he was ever actually required to, as the saying goes, *'terminate with extreme prejudice'*, but he would be aware of such operations and perhaps sanction them. He was evidently extremely active in the methods of extracting information from frequently unwilling victims and was also a keen advocate of what his associates frequently termed as pseudo-science and sometimes simply as 'bullshit'. In fact he had something of the 'X' Files' about him and one can only wonder if the creator of that program, Chris Carter, actually based any of his characters on him. But first we should look a little at the background of the man himself.

Born in 1937, Alexander enjoyed a normal childhood and

joined the US army in 1956. He began a steady and highly qualified career progression before obtaining the rank of full colonel, a position from which he retired in 1988. During his time in the army, Alexander obtained various degrees including a BSc from the University of Nebraska, an MA from Pepperdine University, and in 1980 he attained a PhD for his thesis with the lengthy title of, *'To determine whether or not significant changes in spirituality occur in persons who attended a Kubler-Ross life/death transition workshop during the period June through February 1979'.* Although this paper is somewhat obscure, its subject matter of 'life/death transition' is even more, so it may shed some light on the psyche of the man.

Do not forget that John Alexander was also one of the senior officers in the US army intelligence community that helped promote the concept of an entirely revolutionary form of warfare called the *'1st Earth Battalion'*. This unique idea was first proposed by one Lieutenant Colonel Jim Channon who was another of the people trying to take warfare in another direction designed to appeal directly to the 'hearts and minds' of an enemy rather than roll in with all guns blazing. This involved the use of music and specific sound frequencies designed to create a mental state of calmness, and in some cases involved ostensibly unarmed soldiers advancing toward the enemy carrying lambs. Of course the originators of this process were pragmatic enough to realize that this might not always have the required degree of success; so, as a backstop, the traditional hardware of war was always on hand just in case. It is not clear if this was ever actually deployed as envisioned in the field, but certain elements of it certainly were in the form of loud and discordant music, which this was implemented under the heading of psychological operations, or 'psy-ops'.

The reason that this appealed to Alexander was due to his interest in developing alternative weapons under the new title of 'Non-Lethal Technologies', which was the name of one on the companies he helped found after leaving the army. That is not to say that his duties while in the army were not onerous because they were – he was a commander with the Green Berets and was involved with Special Forces in Vietnam. He also led Cambodian mercenaries operating behind enemy lines and took part in a number of clandestine projects while in this theatre of war. All of this 'hands on' soldering helped feed his desire to find a better way of conducting warfare. One of his abiding interests was, and still is, in anomalous phenomena, i.e. 'the paranormal' and how this might be harnessed for military use.

This included a series of mind control projects initiated by the CIA, which culminated in the infamous and apparently unsuccessful MK-ULTRA. Another of the projects he monitored was the now officially disbanded 'Stargate Project', which involved exotic techniques such as remote viewing. We will return to MK-ULTRA later in the book. Perhaps typically of the man, in 1971 while serving as an infantry Captain at Schofield Barracks in Honolulu, Hawaii, he took part in a series of dives off the Bimini Islands allegedly looking for Atlantis. Bimini is of course where a clairvoyant, the late Edgar Cayce, predicted that fabled city/state would be found. Although there has been no sign of Atlantis either in Bimini, or anywhere else for that matter – although speculation is always rife – one thing that did emerge was the so-called *'Bimini Road'*, which is an enigmatic stretch of apparently paved roadway stretching for some distance below the sea. Incidentally, as recently as 1991 it was reported that Col Alexander was planning to return to the Bimini/Bahamas region to study certain unspecified anomalies.

Admittedly some of the ideas considered by Alexander have proved less than successful, and it is likely that, physical non-lethal weapons aside, they were more intended to promote a specific paradigm rather than be taken literally. These include techniques designed to allow soldiers who had been suitably trained to literally walk through walls, become invisible and read minds. At one point Col Alexander was attached to the US Army Intelligence and Security Command (INSCOM) under the command of General Albert Stubblebine whose remit was to develop the methods necessary to allow this to happen. Perhaps due to the automatic discipline entrained in military thinking the mindset may be extremely literal, which is why these methods were attempted. It may seem rather odd and requires a measure of lateral thinking, but one can almost understand why a human being might actually be able to pass through a solid object. At first sight the theory seems impossible, but on closer inspection achievable. A solid object, say a wall or door, consists of atoms and even smaller particles existing at specific frequencies; the person also consists of frequencies vibrating at more or less the same rate, it's why the wall or door acts as a barrier.

If one could somehow change the frequency of the person or the obstacle then, the theory goes, they should be able to pass through the solid object, simple, right? Well no, it is not, quite apart from their not being able to make it work, logically, if the person did somehow alter their bodily frequency to pass through a solid object, then the floor (or ground) would no longer support them and they would simply fall through the Earth. The same applied to another project, that of invisibility: the assumption was again, literally, that the person should be transparent, effectively an invisible man. But this could not be made to work either. Since the inspiration for this seems to come from exotic martial arts techniques, the idea was not to become literally invisible, rather it was to develop the art of not being seen. The title, *'Ninjitsu'*, from which we derive the term *'Ninja'*, translates directly as *'the art of not being seen'*, which is entirely appropriate considering that the Ninja were a type of assassin who, ideally, would not want to be seen.

The range of non-lethal technologies reportedly considered by Alexander include electromagnetic weapons, chemical options like *'sticky foam'*, different kinds of restraint including *'net guns'* that project a sheet of webbing (sometimes electrified) over an assailant and acoustic weapons like *'curdlers'*, which were acoustic devices designed to emit vomit inducing frequencies. There was another experimental device in a similar vein produced for the purpose of producing *'brown noise'*, this was intended to cause those affected by the frequencies to spontaneously and uncontrollably empty their bowels. Yet another electronic weapon was a very powerful microwave emitter to cause an intense burning sensation on the skin of anyone standing within its range. Also in the arsenal are *'information weapons'*, which are longer term and almost certainly include disinformation etc., and finally, non-lethal biological weapons, including quick acting toxins and substances that, like the 'brown noise' transducers, act as extremely effective and rapid laxatives.

Other organizations that Col Alexander became involved with that at first sight had no obvious military application include *'The National Institute for Discovery Science'* or NIDS for short, which was founded in 1995 by a Las Vegas based Millionaire called Robert Bigelo, who is also a very close friend of Alexander. NIDS exists to investigate various phenomena currently described as 'paranormal' and this includes everything from UFOs and ETs to poltergeists. Although the NIDS website is still active there have been no new postings since 2004 and it is believed that the group is no longer active. Prior to this he became an advisor to, and apparently still is, of *'The Appolinaire Group'*, yet another Las Vegas-based organization whose purpose is the study of anomalous and paranormal phenomena. In this group, which was set up in 1982, Col Alexander is referred to as 'Dr Alexander', which is as it should be due to the simple fact that he received a doctorate from one of the universities he attended.

The name of the Appolinaire Group seems to derive from the poet Guillaume Appolinaire, the assumed name of the inventor of the term 'surrealist', which describes the artistic movement that spawned such luminaries as Salvador Dali, Jean Cocteau,

Marc Chagall, Gertrude Stein and Pablo Picasso. One of Appolinaire's less savory claims to fame came when he was accused of stealing the Mona Lisa. He was released without charge after a week, but while in custody pointed the finger at Picasso who was also questioned but later released; whether their friendship continued after this is doubtful. Quite why Appolinaire's name was chosen to front an organization investigating anomalous phenomena is unclear but it may be connected to the unique nature of the style of art that he helped create. At present Col Alexander still lives with his wife in Las Vegas, although he did spend approximately four months during 2004 in Afghanistan acting as a 'special advisor' involving non-lethal methods used in extracting information from suspects. This involved such techniques as placing the subject blindfolded in a cargo container and bombarding them with loud rock music for hours on end; the outcome of these techniques is unknown.

Col Alexander still maintains an interest in his hobbies and still actively participates in the activities of the organizations of which he is a member, and he will still answer sensible emails sent to him. His office address in Las Vegas is that of the now defunct NIDS, which may be an indication that it is not as inactive as it first appears. If this is the case it should come as no surprise, because Col Alexander is still a man of vast experience with many secrets locked in his head and is obviously still in demand by his government. My own dealings with Col Alexander were by email and connected to my own research concerning the maverick inventor John Hutchison and I found him to be polite and to the point. As far as I can gather he believes that the Hutchison Effect is a genuine if elusive phenomenon; he attributes it to 'Macro-PK' (psychokinesis), or the ability to either cause objects to move by an act of will or in some other way influence them. This may be so, but my own investigations indicate that there had to be a specific set of circumstances in place, including the presence of wide range of electromagnetic fields before this anomaly will occur and significantly Hutchison has to be present. If the Colonel and the LANL scientists saw the effect manifest in Hutchison's laboratory it is fair to assume that they wanted it to work repeatedly – and to order – and become part of the weird and wonderful arsenal hidden in the secrecy of the 'black world'.

Although ostensibly promoting the reality of paranormal phenomena, Col Alexander was (and as with his many other interests indeed may still be) part of a group collectively known as 'The Aviary'. This organization was set up to act as a disinformation source dealing with the vexed issue of UFOs, and each of the members was known by the name of a bird, which in Col Alexander's case was 'Penguin'. Other members of the clandestine group included Dr. Harold Puthoff, known as 'Owl', and a member of the influential 'Stanford Research Institute', (SRI), an organization that was closely involved with the CIA's remote viewing 'Stargate Project' and other exotic concepts. Interestingly, Puthoff was also a close associate of Dr. Russell Targ, yet another member of the SRI who was also involved in the remote viewing venture. Other Aviary associates were Dr Jack Verona, a US Department of Defense (DOD) employee who was also instrumental in the 'Sleeping Beauty' project. This idea, which was bankrolled by the Defense Intelligence Agency, was intended to develop electromagnetic weapons capable of exerting a negative influence over (presumably) enemy soldiers in the battle zone. Also included was the CIA's Dr Christopher Green known as 'Bluejay' and Dr Ron Gandolphi, a physicist working at the Rocket and Missile section of the Office of the Deputy Director of Science and Technology, CIA, who was called 'Pelican'.

One of the notable successes, if that is the correct term, achieved by this group was the complete mental breakdown of the unfortunate Dr Paul Bennewitz. Bennewitz's downfall came about at the hands of a former UFO researcher named William

Moore who had been 'turned' by The Aviary with the promise of inside information on the UFO enigma. In return for this so-called 'information' Moore was instructed to feed disinformation supplied by members of The Aviary to selected individuals, in particular Paul Bennewitz. This may well have been due to the fact that Dr Bennewitz had a quantity of film showing events unfolding in the sky above a weapons storage area at Kirtland Airforce base during the 1980's. The steady input of lies and half-truths, which the trusting Bennewitz accepted at face value, eventually cast serious doubt on the rest of the evidence he had gathered and caused him to look particularly foolish to the rest of the UFO community. Understandably this had a serious effect on his self-confidence and reputation, so much so that he was eventually committed to a psychiatric institution.

Chapter 9
Austin Osman Spare

Although a noted and gifted artist, Spare was also a Chaos Magician who, as well as almost single-handedly defining the concept of Chaos Magic, practiced a mystical system called *'Kiaism'* which does not seem to have affiliations with any other tradition of magic and seems to infer that the practitioner creates his own magical methodology. This is exactly what Chaos Magic is all about and allows the magician to operate the system according to their own ideas providing the appropriate results are obtained. Spare was repeatedly asked to define what his system was and how it worked, but he insisted that it could not be defined and any attempt to do so rendered it more obscure. This explanation, such as it is, tempts one to speculate that even he may not have been sure how it worked. In addition, Spare developed the ancient practice and use of Sigils to a fine art. Sigils are formed when, for example, a spell, irrespective of purpose, is written out in its entirety then gradually 'stripped down' until only one symbol comprising elements (normally individual letters) from the entire spell are left; if done correctly this is considered to possess great latent power. The same process of compression can also be used to concentrate an entire book down to a single figure, if this was applied to a work such as a grimoire (a book of spells), the resulting sigil might have terrifying potential.

However, the use of sigils and their preparation, as befits Chaos Magic, has never been precisely defined and left up the idiosyncrasies of the user; but as already stated, they represent the very nub and core of the intent and as such they have considerable latent power. One quite well known list of 72 ancient sigils was in a volume called the *'Lesser Key of Solomon'*, sometimes referred to as *'The Lemegeton'*. This particular work uses a system of magic called *'The Goetia'*, which translates as 'howling', and refers to the manner in which the incantations are used. The magician literally shrieks the words as each spell is read trying to elevate themselves into an ecstatic state, which seems to mirror the techniques associated with Chaos Magic. Once again it makes one wonder whether the spell is effective irrespective of the conjuration, relying instead on the sheer will and desire of the magician, or if the form of the words is also important.

Each sigil referred to one individual demon and was regarded as its secret name; possession of these sigils gave the magician power over whatever demon was called. Interestingly, it is known that the semi-legendary King Solomon of the bible was regarded as a demonologist and magician of note who controlled 40 demonic entities in the construction of his temple using sigils. At one point Spare created a 'sigil alphabet' called *'The Sacred Alphabet'* or, the *'Alphabet of Desire'* and it is important to realize that in this context there is no inference of equating desire with sex, rather, it means 'will' or 'intent'. Strangely enough this is one point of convergence with Crowley's practice of *'Thelema'*, a word that translates directly as 'will'.

Having mentioned alphabets, while recording their results etc, many magicians who acted on advice contained in a volume on magic called the *'Grimorium Verum'*, took the precaution of writing with ink taken from inkwells inscribed with the following words of protection, **'Yod'**, **'He'**, **'Vau'**, **'He'**, **'Metatron'**, **'Yod'**, **'Cados'**, **'Eloym'**, **'Sabaoth'**, where 'Metatron' was the name of the angel who acted as a guide for the Israelites during their time in the wilderness. The name is also fully interchangeable with *'Shaddai'* (Almighty), because in 'Gematria', the practice of divination by substituting letters for numbers, both words total 314. 'Cados' is the Hebrew version of *'Kadosh'* or 'Holy One', yet another and obvious title given to God. This may have the same relevance as wearing medals bearing an image of St Christopher, the patron saint of travelers, when undertaking a journey and is also found in the practice of having an item blessed by a priest to ensure the safety of its wearer or user. It is the same rationale behind the traditional naming ceremony of a ship with the words, *'May God bless her and all who sail in her'* – a clear invocation to a higher power to protect the vessel.

The practice of Gematria and the closely related technique called *'Numerology'*, dates back for millennia and it is still relatively common today; and the manner in which words and phrases of similar meaning, especially those found in the Old and New Testaments, have identical numerical values is genuinely astonishing. One is almost tempted to speculate, and with good reason, that language is an artificial construct designed around mathematical principles. This is found in the English language, which as well as constantly evolving, is noted for its careful and incredibly subtle nuances. Hebrew is another language that works well with Gematria and indeed, in terms of age, orthodox Jews are quick to point out that Hebrew was the common language of both men and angels. It may also be the reason that many ancient treatises on magic use this language. This is a concept that is far from new and it can be argued that the entire multiverse and all it contains are likewise based on mathematical foundations. In fact the late, great, Sir Isaac Newton (1642-1727) memorably said that, *'The universe is a cryptogram set by the Almighty'*, which in turn invites the question, if by extension it was not a Creator God that created life on earth then what was it?

Sigils are not always necessarily visual and can also be in the form of sounds and sensory impressions such as smells and tactile impressions. The concept of sonic sigils is entirely logical: if the visual sigil is the essence of a desire, then the sonic sigil may be the quintessence of a spoken desire expressed as music that is gradually whittled down to a final musical chord or even a single tone or frequency. The reasoning is exactly the same, the reduction of something down to a condensed version of the same thing. This may have been done using certain works of art that contain hidden or occult meanings; such an artifact is called a *'hypersigil'* and has immense potential power; it is a custom that finds expression in certain runes still used in pagan ceremonies. Traces of the custom continued in the 'mason marks' used by the early guilds of stonemasons who traveled around Europe plying their trade in the cathedrals and other major medieval building projects. The individual mark of each tradesman was frequently composed of their names or initials reproduced in a single intricate shape, usually a pleasing and harmonious design. It was his own sigil and a unique identifier quite different from that of their brother craftsman; it is a custom that still persists today in the *'Mark Master Degree'* worked in Masonic lodges the world over.

To further define the use of sigils as words or tones, if this definition was applied to a single word, then it is logical to assume that these sounds may have been used as the so-called 'words of power' wielded by the magicians and prophets of old. Take for example the letters compromising the *'Shemhamforash'*, or 'pre-eminent name', a word consisting of 72 syllables allegedly used by Moses to separate the Red Sea. The word itself derives from the Book of Exodus by taking three of its verses, each containing 72 letters to create a further 72 three letter names of God. The use of the word was also used in the manufacture of a *'Golem'*, the terrifying artificial being of legend in the Jewish faith. The tale of the Golem might also be seen as an analogy based on the creation of the first man, Adam, because according to scriptural tradition Adam was created from dust into which God breathed life and the Golem is also created in the main from earth then activated using the real name of God.

This word was of such immense power that even one mistake in its pronunciation could blast the wielder to ashes and vaporize the surrounding area. The word has since been lost or forgotten, which upon reflection is perhaps just as well. Another word allegedly possessing amazing power and used by magicians is the *'Tetragrammaton'*. This word, which is in fact what the Shemhamforash represents, is claimed to be the ineffable, (or secret *and personal*) name of God. The word is usually represented by the letters YHVH, which are the Hebrew initials of the words YOD, HEY, VAU, HEY, and is usually pronounced as 'Yahweh'. The substitution of 'Yahweh' is due to the likelihood of severe damage caused by the misuse of the real or personal name of God by speaking it out loud; according to tradition even thinking it is extremely dangerous. This might also provide a link with Freemasonry where one of the words currently in use is a substitute for the original, which was lost or forgotten in the mists of antiquity. Once again, as with the name of God, it is peculiar how ancient beliefs, rites and ceremonies appear to share the same or similar roots. In fact in some of the more fundamentalist Christian beliefs even writing the word 'God' is strongly disapproved of, and if it must be reproduced at all then a letter is missed out as in G-d.

In these same beliefs, if it was to be spoken, it was done so almost inaudibly using the softest of whispers. Perhaps a resonance of this is, once again, still found in Freemasonry where a certain part of the rituals specifically refers to secret words that are spoken only *'at low breath'*, or in other words in a whisper. This is particularly true of the 'mason word' itself, which is imparted to the candidate during the 'Third Degree', a term that has slipped into common usage and describes particularly intense and frequently robust interrogations. Also of interest is the synchronous use of the number 72 in relation to magical words, which also appears in the number of archangels who stand guard against the powers of darkness. Curiously, it is also of significance to practitioners of the Cabala because the value of the letters, YHVH, in Cabbalism is 72, and as previously mentioned it was coincidentally also the age at which Aleister Crowley died. The repeated reference to numbers in relation to the name of God again finds relevance in the number four, which is of particular magical significance since it is the number of letters in the personal name of God, and – even more significantly – was the name/word/sound used to create the universe. This is of course rather different from the Buddhist version of events, which is mentioned a little later, where the sound (or word) is 'OM'. The main thing here is that sound, ergo frequency, in one manner or another was present to trigger the beginning of existence.

While on this subject it is relevant to mention that God has been known by a number of names, among them, *'Shaddi'*, *'Adonai'*, *'Jehovah'*, *'Elohim'*, *'Eloa'*, *'Saboath'* and several other titles all of which refer to 'a God', although the most potent of all of them is, as we have seen, the Tetragrammaton. The practise of not using personal names when referring to a supreme deity also gained general acceptance at a more mundane level in many societies where the use of one's own name by a stranger was considered to give the user a degree of power over the person whose name it was. Something similar is found even today in cultures where individuals are still uneasy about having their picture taken in case they lose some of their 'life essence', or soul.

Another example of the use of words of power appears as recently as the first quarter of the 20th century in Saudi Arabia where the introduction of radio broadcasting aroused considerable suspicion among the deeply conservative and superstitious Muslim clergy. They thought that in some way the use of radio was Satanic and originally refused to sanction its use; it was not until it was used to transmit the name of Allah that they were persuaded that if it was unholy in nature it could not possibly have carried the name of the Supreme Being. This is a prime example of the church and state being as one, although, to be fair, the country, despite being still closely monitored by the Sunni Wahabbist religious authorities, has become slightly less restrictive.

Not surprisingly Spare, the son of a London policeman, moved in the same circles as Crowley and joined his recently established 'Argenteum Astrum' as a probationer, but was never fully accepted. Crowley called him a 'Black Brother' and disliked his magical philosophy; this may well have been because Spare did not care for the pomp and theatrics of Crowley's highly ritualized ceremonies, instead preferring the more intimate nature of his own interpretation. Another clear difference between them, and indeed the majority of those who followed the type of elitist mysticism espoused by Crowley and his ilk, was the fact that Spare was unashamedly working class.

On the other hand, Crowley's social circles consisted in the main of an intelligentsia who affected literary and artistic airs and graces, and Spare was never entirely at ease with them. It is also possible that 'The Beast' did not like anyone whose talents may have been a threat to his own reputation. The most notable contribution made by Osman Spare to the lexicon of the occult was the concept of *'Self Love'*, which, it should be made clear from the outset, was not any narcissistic pandering to inflated ego, but was, instead, a mental state similar to that produced by an expression of joy, like laughter. This mental state allegedly permits the expansion of consciousness, soul if you like, to embrace freedom of expression without definition. It is strangely resonant and consistent with Spare's fundamental refusal, or perhaps that might be inability, to define his magical system.

Chapter 10
Kenneth Grant

Although by no means the last, one of the most recent magicians worthy of note is Kenneth Grant who was, at the time of writing, still alive. Like many of the people mentioned in this section, Grant knew Crowley and Spare and no doubt many of the others who were around at the time. It would be difficult not to, since the brotherhood to which they all belonged was, to say the least, both rarefied and exclusive. As with Spare, Grant was a member of the Argenteum Astrum, but went on to become a full member and later joined the OTO. Such was his enthusiasm and talent that in 1946, Crowley, who was by now approaching the end of his life, decided that should he die, Grant was qualified and well suited to take over running the OTO in the UK, and as it transpired this is exactly what happened. Following Crowley's death in 1947 Grant was elevated to high office in the OTO and this was accepted by Karl Germer the then head of the Order. In 1951 Grant stated that he was then authorized to lead and run the OTO in England and proceeded to inject some much needed energy into the Order by creating new degrees.

Not content to lie back on his laurels, and in the spirit of its founder, Grant began to put some of his own ideas in motion by founding his own group, the *'New Isis Lodge'*, which became fully operational in 1955. Due to Grant's discovery of what he called a *'Sirius/Set current'*, the new organization incurred the displeasure of Germer, who was the European head of the OTO and nominally the head of the OTO worldwide. This rift culminated in Grant's expulsion from the OTO, but undeterred Grant declared himself 'Outer Head' of the OTO, a schism that became generally known as the '*Typhonian Ordo Templi Orientis*'. A little later, in 1962, Grant's 'New Isis Lodge' merged seamlessly with his version of the OTO, an act that greatly increasing his influence in occult circles.

Grant and the previously mentioned Osman Spare became good friends, which lead to the creation of the '*Zos Kia Cultus*', an organization that seems to have been influenced by Spare's magical philosophy. So close did they become that Grant went out of his way to promote Spare's artistic and occult interests where he could and brought his name to prominence in many western magical circles. The friendship results in Grant becoming Spares' biographer. Although the practice of magic still exists, it is more as a factor of witchcraft and is the subject of a considerable lack of knowledge and deep prejudice in the popular press. Unfortunately these media reports mainly derive from the dabbling of amateurs who have no real understanding of what they are doing or the potential for great harm they incur, and for the most part the bad press is richly deserved. The downside of course is the damage that is done to serious practitioners who have no interest in murdering animals or despoiling graveyards, especially since none of it is required other than for effect or to pander to the ego of the individual.

Chapter 11
Anton Szandor LaVey

The character and motivation of Anton Szandor LaVey is, perhaps, more easily defined and exemplifies the sea change in attitudes that took place in society during the years following the Second World War. Born Howard Stanton LaVey in 1924, he was an ex high school dropout who began his career working as a general laborer in fairs and carnivals and later displayed some talent as a musician playing the organ in bars, nightclubs and lounges. He is a prime example of the old maxim that, '*If you want to make money found a religion*', and that is exactly what he went on to do, although, like Crowley, his 'religion' was not exactly conventional.

One of the biggest, and it has to be said self-proclaimed, influences on his choice of 'faith' seems to have derived from the blatant hypocrisy demonstrated by the men he encountered who attended and leered at the Saturday night burlesque performances where he worked, then appeared complete with their families clutching their bibles the following Sunday morning at the evangelical Christian, revivalist, tub thumping tent shows. A word of warning here, LaVey was alleged to have repeatedly massaged his personal history with the addition of various aspects that suited his agenda and promoted his choices, so it is best to keep an open mind regarding some of his background.

Following his musical beginnings he allegedly worked as a police department photographer in San Francisco and also set himself up as a psychic investigator; although there are no records showing that he had ever worked for the police force, his claims of psychic investigations carry more weight. One thing that did bring him a measure of fame were his paranormal investigations and performances as an organist, and he attracted several notables such as the noted science fiction writer, Fritz Leiber, and the magazine editor and Sci-Fi buff Forrest J. Ackerman. Another recruit was the previously mentioned outré film director Kenneth Anger, who, as we have seen, was also an alleged magician. In the early 1960's LaVey hosted a series of Friday night lectures focusing on occult subjects for a like-minded group that he called his 'Magic Circle'.

This led to one of the group suggesting that he use it as a springboard to set up a religion, and on the 30th of April 1966, (Walpurgisnacht), he shaved his head during a ritual and pronounced the inauguration of *'The Church of Satan'*, declaring 1966 as 'The Year One', or as he had it, *'Anno Satanas'* (Satan's Year). This type of chronological indulgence and/or conceit is not new, and has had unthinkable consequences for those unfortunate enough to suffer its consequences in, for example, South East Asia during the murderous regime of the vicious and power-drunk demagogue, Pol Pot. This cancer on the soul of humanity resulted in an ideological holocaust of dogma that led in the deaths of tens of thousands of innocents as the unspeakable Pol Pot, through the agency of the Khmer Rouge, attempted to enforce his warped politics on a terrified population and created what became known as *'The Killing Fields'*. The film of the same name precisely depicts the systematic cruelty practiced by those who blindly followed the blinkered delusions of Pol Pot's evil master plan manifested through his hideous ideological apocalypse. Although not known as followers of any dark forces, like many before them through the ages there can be little doubt that the actions of the Khmer Rouge would find favor with any entities that feed of the maelstrom of terror generated by their cruelty. Fortunately Pol Pot is now dead.

During the 1960's and 70's LaVey's 'church' attracted other Hollywood symbols such as Jayne Mansfield, (who was beheaded in a car crash) and others on the Hollywood 'B' list. In addition he carried out various Satanic weddings, Satanic baptisms and Satanic funerals. At one point in the early 1950's he also claimed to have had an affair with the then unknown Marilyn Monroe, something that has been strongly repudiated by associates of that unfortunate and much put upon actress. Perhaps LaVey's most notable contribution to occult lore was his book, *'The Satanic Bible'*, which has been produced in several editions and has seldom been out of print since its first publication. This work is a curious mixture of concepts, ideas, imprecations, invocations and philosophy interspersed with lines and abstruse verses transcribed in the Enochian language and the mixture made to fit LaVey's personal agenda. Like most of its predecessors it is evidently required to shock and mortify those who do not accept it's 'new' revelations of freedom, and once again, like its forbears, this seemingly needs copious amounts of gratuitous sex and nudity. The desire to shock seems irrevocably married to the need to be 'different' or 'new' and may only be a crude device designed to attract attention, notoriety and, of course, ever welcome free publicity. Like nearly all of those who follow a magical path he felt it necessary to enhance his status by adopting a title, in this case 'Doctor'.

Unfortunately and perhaps inevitably, as with many sensational books of this kind, it has filtered its way into the subculture of loners, misfits and others who, for whatever reason, feel rejected by mainstream society and find solace and acceptance in the promotion of rebellion and denial of conformity within its covers. Taken on one level it can be read fairly dispassionately for what it is, a cynical ploy to make money and promote hedonism wrapped around a central core of occult musings and formulae derived from a range of sources. Much more dangerously it can also be viewed as a manual with which to bring about widespread chaos though the application of totally misunderstood principles relating to personal freedom. This is based on another of LaVey's dictums concerning the rejection of responsibility and conscience in the pursuit of pleasure and power.

It could be argued that he tried to embrace at least part of Crowley's motto of, *'Do what thou wilt shall be the whole of the law'* and this is an extremely risky path to take because *'Do what you wilt'* is not the same as *'Do what thou like'*. If nothing else we have all to obey the law of the land and observe a measure of control, especially regarding the laws governing the taking of human life, and this is where a very few of his unofficial followers got it badly and terribly wrong. It is also the same ballpark nihilistic philosophy that obsessed people like Charles Manson and his unpleasant 'family' of the inadequate and socially addled rejects who developed in the drug soaked culture of the 1960s. This of course led directly to the pointless and tragic murder of the pregnant actress Sharon Tate and her friends by those under the influence of the lunatic logic employed by Manson. This evil act, which we will return to later, has continued to reverberate as a stark reminder of what happens when society undergoes upheaval and experiences new and unaccustomed freedom. To be fair to LaVey, he does make it very clear that the sacrifice of human beings, and infants in particular, is not the driving force behind his version of Satan worship and is in effect negative propaganda put out by the Catholic Church to exclude Satanism from the mainstream.

LaVey's ideology was an amalgam derived in the main from the nihilism of Friedrich Nietzsche and the writings and philosophies of the aforementioned Aleister Crowley. In his opinion Crowley, although talented, was for the most part a poseur, and while some of this may be true it cannot be denied that Crowley certainly thought of himself as a major player in the world of the occult and his followers thought so too, but there may have been another reason for LaVey's rather biased view. For example, he considered that his own version of Satanism was a pure form of worship and he was clear that it did not involve the so-called 'Black Mass', going so far as to state that this was not the ceremony used by genuine Satanists. He quite rightly points out that the Black Mass is intended as a parody of the service used by the Catholic Church while what he did was not. Oddly enough, the same argument can be used about parodying any religious service, Catholic or not, and, as we saw earlier, Crowley was sometimes at considerable pains to protest that he did not worship Satan. This brings about an odd dichotomy in the philosophy of LaVey: on the one hand while vehemently castigating so-called 'white magic' and 'white magicians' as virtually worthless, by inference he must have regarded himself as a 'black magician', yet he claims not to have practiced 'black magic' *per se*.

Another ancient mage whose writings greatly influenced LaVey was the medieval polymath and alchemist, Dr John Dee, a man of immense talent and intellect and inventor of the Enochian language through which he claimed to communicate with 'angels', the name he gave to the entities he communicated with through the agency of various 'scrying glasses'. These were optical devices that allowed the user to concentrate and focus rather in the manner of using a crystal ball. This analogy, although it will serve, is not 100% accurate, because according to Dee and his assistant, Edward Kelley, these artefacts allowed actual glimpses of sights normally denied to ordinary men; they were effectively glimpsing other dimensions. LaVey was one of those astute enough to realize that what Dee supposedly saw through his scrying lenses may not have been angels at all, but, instead, 'angles', the frightening geometry of an alien dimension. In addition, some descriptions of these artefacts describe them as made of 'obsidian', a volcanic glass that is sometimes black and occasionally green. Other descriptions say that they were crystal, but whatever the material their function was identical.

Actually, when one studies the life of John Dee, who, as we have already seen, used the code, '007' as one of his aliases, one discovers that there was considerably more to the man than his interest in magic. Along with Sir Francis Walsingham he helped set up the British secret service and it has been suggested that the Enochian language was, in fact, a cipher used to send messages to and from the fledgling secret service. He was also a confidante of Queen Elizabeth I and through her protection and patronage managed to avoid the predations of the religious authorities who still enjoyed considerable influence in the government of the country. Do not forget that at this time in history, witches and warlocks, a definition that adequately described Dee's lifestyle, were persecuted, tortured and put to death on a regular basis using a variety of means. Nevertheless, in spite of his obvious connections, intelligence and learning, when Dee eventually reached the end of his life it was in relative penury and he died in poverty with his earlier successes a distant memory.

Throughout his life LaVey never flinched from promoting either his lifestyle or 'Church', and like most of his ilk reveled in his lifestyle. He was a regular guest on various radio and TV programs and of course graced the pages of popular magazines. In addition he adapted the 'Enochian Keys', devised and decoded by the previously mentioned Dr John Dee, into a modernized version designed for use in his 'bible', spells and other published works. When he finally died in 1997, ironically he was taken to a Roman Catholic hospital; but by some strange coincidence, although he died on the 29th of October, his death was entered as two days later, on the 31st October, Halloween. Another magical practitioner named Zeena Schrek claimed to have killed him by calling down a curse, the reason why is unknown, but may have been due to some insult either real or imagined. Following his cremation at a very private, not to say secret, ceremony, his ashes, which were assumed to possess great occult power, were divided among his heirs for use in rituals.

Before leaving the subject of LaVey, it might be informative to examine some of the characters that he drew to him. At the time when LaVey's star was on the ascendant, as mentioned elsewhere, there was a great cultural upheaval in society: it was the 1960's, the Second World War and the conflict with Korea had ended and society experienced a great awakening in its ideas and cultural norms. Although these armed conflicts have evaporated, the Cold War was now well established and the population was fatigued by the paranoia and the threats. It was a time of rebellion, it was a time of change and experimentation and the effects of recreational drugs were making inroads into the outlook and values of the young. Even the traditional and conservative values of religion in the United States were losing ground to a desire for expression.

Chapter 12
Charles Manson

Although not in the same league as the others so far mentioned, it is reasonable to include Manson, a career criminal, and the unsavory reputation surrounding both him and his followers. Perhaps they, more than any other group other than politically motivated terrorist organizations like *'The Weathermen'*, the *'Simbionese Liberation Army'*, who famously captured and apparently indoctrinated the heiress, Patty Hurst, and the European *'Bader-Meinhoff Group'*, came to typify just how the 1960s changed forever the way society thought and behaved, and not necessarily for the better. Charles Mills Manson first saw the light of day on the 12th of November 1934 in Cincinnati Ohio and was the youngest of four children along with Luther, Joanne and Kathleen.

His father, Charles Maddox left his mother, Kathleen, shortly after learning that she was pregnant with her latest child. Perhaps there was a hint of what was to come stemming from both his birth parents: his father, who was an unskilled laborer, adopted the unlikely military title of 'Colonel Scott', and his mother, Kathleen, had run away from home at fifteen due to the pressures of living with her fundamentalist Christian parents. The name, Manson, originates from his stepfather, William Manson, a man considerably older than Kathleen, with whom she lived shortly after the birth of her son. Incidentally, the adoption of the title, 'Colonel', by Charlie's natural father is no more odd than the use of the same entirely unjustified rank by Tom Parker, the former manager of the late Elvis Presley.

As if his choices were not already limited, Charlie's fortunes were further diminished, when at the age of six, his mother and uncle robbed a service station in Charleston in West Virginia at gunpoint, leading to their subsequent arrest and imprisonment for five years. During this time Charlie went to live with his aunt, Joanne, and her husband, Bill, and this seems to have been one of the very few periods of stability in young Charlie's life. However, when his mother was released from prison they lived a fairly nomadic life, drifting from town to town in various states including Ohio, Indiana, Kentucky and West Virginia, always on the verge of destitution. During this unsettling period Charlie mutely watched his mother take various 'boy friends', something that he later admitted upset him greatly.

Eventually Charlie discovered that he had a talent for music and, to some extent, both singing and song writing – something that he was more than happy to exploit – and in the few years prior to the formation of the 'family' he had some modest success, although the 'big time' always eluded him. As the 1960's began, along with most people of his age he embraced the counterculture that developed around the philosophy of 'free love' and drugs and due to his natural charisma Charlie developed into a type of blue collar guru attracting a loose following. At its height his family, which was in actuality a hippie commune, consisted of approximately thirty-two members, but only twenty-two of them are known and these include those who carried out the murders of the actress Sharon Tate and her friends. The murderers, who took a total of six lives in the Tate home, were Charles Watson, Linda Kasabian, Susan Atkins and Patricia Krenwinkle.

What makes the deaths even more outlandish was the fact that Sharon Tate's husband, Roman Polanski, who was in the United Kingdom at the time of the murders, had just recently completed directing the Satanic horror film, *Rosemary's Baby*, (1968) which had Anton LaVey as its technical advisor. During the slaughter, which was carried out with guns and knives, the hippies, who had already adopted the name, *'The Creepy Crawlies'*, daubed the word, 'Pigs', on the front door using Sharon Tate's blood. The following night and once again with no apparent motive other than Manson's warped philosophy, the Creepy Crawlies struck again, this time murdering a middle-aged couple, Rosemary and Leno LeBianca. This time the words, 'Rise', 'Death to Pigs' and *'Healter Skelter'* (sic) were daubed on the walls of the house written using the blood of the victims. Again the word, 'War', was used, but this time carved into the chest of Leno LeBianca who also had a knife and fork stuck into his stomach.

In 1975 yet another of Manson's grotesque 'family' achieved infamy when Lynette (squeaky) Fromme walked up to former US president, Gerald Ford as if to shake hands, but instead pulled out a pistol, pointed it at him and pulled the trigger. Fortunately the gun was not loaded. Fromme later stated that she had no intention of killing the president, but was later given a life sentence for her stupidity. Recent presidents John F. Kennedy and Ronald Regan were less fortunate; but Ronald Regan at least survived the attempt on his life. John Hinckley perpetrated the attempt to assassinate Regan in 1981 after he had been in office for just 69 days. As he emerged from a speaking engagement in a Washington hotel, Regan and three others were shot and wounded by Hinckley. The reason for the attack was, astonishingly, that Hinckley through his infatuation, wanted to impress the actress Jodie Foster. He was found insane and committed to a secure psychiatric hospital where he still remains to this day.

Chapter 13
Bobby Beausoleil

One more major player in the sordid Manson saga was another small time musician and would be actor, Robert Kenneth (Bobby) Beausoleil, who almost achieved the same notoriety as Manson himself. Born in 1947 in Santa Barbara California, the young Bobby attracted little interest other than his ambition to break into the world of music and the lifestyle that it afforded. Although his primary interest was in the music scene, he also thought that his good looks would bring him better rewards in the world of cinema and to that end he agreed to appear in Kenneth Anger's *Lucifer Rising*, and it is here that we see many strands coming together.

Although starting out with good intentions it was not long before Beausoleil and Anger fell out and the entire project was shelved, although some of the footage appeared in another of Anger's projects, a film called *Invocation of My Demon Brother.* Not surprisingly Crowley's philosophy was well known to Manson and his group, and it was during the 1960s that the deceased magician enjoyed a considerable renaissance. It was also alleged that when Beausoleil and Anger went their separate ways, Beausoleil, in a fit of pique, took most of the completed film with him and buried it in the desert close to one of Manson's former hideouts.

Beausoleil's main claim to infamy however is his association with Manson's unsavory 'family' and the 1969 murder of a disc jockey called Gary Hinman. On the night of the murder Beausoleil was accompanied by Susan Atkins and Mary Brunner and arrived at Hinman's house to reclaim property and money that Manson claimed was owed to the 'family'. However, according to Beausoleil the murder was over a batch of poor quality mescaline, a well-known traditional hallucinogen supplied by Hinman and sold on by the family to a gang of Hells Angels called, 'The Straight Satans'. When the bikers asked for their money back, Manson, who was well aware of the dangers of upsetting the Hells Angels, promptly sent Beausoleil and the others to Hinman who refused to pay. After repeated refusals, Manson appeared on the scene and attacked Hinman with a knife slashing his face and ear in the process. The torture ended the following day when Beausoleil stabbed Hinman to death, then wrote the words, 'Political Piggy,' on one of the walls using Hinman's blood. In 1970, Beausoleil was sentenced to death, but this was later commuted to life imprisonment in 1972 when the California Supreme Court ruled that the death penalty was unconstitutional. It is probably as well that the American justice system has a complex appeals system that can drag on for many years in relation to murder charges; otherwise Beausoleil would have been long gone.

There have been a few specious attempts to link the actions of Manson and his family to the mythology surrounding the legendary band, The Beatles. It has been suggested that the song, *'Helter Skelter'*, was in some way a tribute to the murders and that another track, *'Piggies'*, contains the words 'forks and knives' and 'eating bacon'. Whether or not this has any basis in fact is dubious, but, as with the furor surrounding the picture on the Beatles album, *Abbey Road*, showing the band walking on a Zebra Crossing with Paul McCartney out of step with the rest of the band, (because he was out of step it was suggested that he was in fact dead), it appears to one of the hazards associated with celebrity and conspiracy.

Chapter 14
Kenneth Anger

In many ways Anger, through his fascination with and knowledge of the occult, was not a man to be trifled with. Born Kenneth Wilbur Anglemyer, the surname, 'Anger,' being adopted later for reasons of image, he began making films at the tender age of nine. The first of his works to achieve attention was a Los Angeles filmed 1947 release called *Fireworks,* which caught the eye of the French director and artist, Jean Cocteau, a man not unconnected with occult subjects. He was invited to Paris where he collaborated with Cocteau on a few projects, and it was in Paris several years later, in 1959, that he achieved his reputation through the publication of a book entitled *Hollywood Babylon.* This publication, which almost became a cult, was a remarkably frank account of the dark and sordid underbelly of the American film world. It was the sort of work that hooked its reader with an almost sick and hypnotic fascination, so much so that the film studios, which obviously had vested interests to protect, made various attempts to prevent its publication. This meant that the book was not officially released in the USA until 1974, although an unofficial and incomplete version had first surfaced in 1965.

From his formative years Anger became fascinated with the magick of Aleister Crowley and adopted Crowley's concept of *'Thelema'* as his religion in his mid-teens. In 1955 Anger traveled to Cefalu in Sicily where he made a documentary film at the ruins of Crowley's Thelema Abbey; it is unknown what became of this work and is now considered as 'lost'. In the 1960's Anger also was associated with the celebrated band, The Rolling Stones, through his casting of Mick Jagger's then girlfriend, Marianne Faithful, in the previously mentioned *Lucifer Rising*.

Anger's long association with the occult in all its forms inevitably brought him into contact with a variety of bizarre groups including that of Anton LaVey with whom he formed an enduring bond both before and after LaVey founded his 'Church of Satan'. At one point in the 1980s Anger actually lived for a time with LaVey and his family and more recently became a member of the OTO. From then until the beginning of the new millennium he largely dropped out of filmmaking, but since then has returned to a subject that he really loved and understood, although both now and in the past his work has yet to find a wide audience.

Chapter 15
Military Intelligence and the Occult

So far we have seen that for some reason there is an almost natural attraction between the covert agencies charged with guarding our freedom and security – the military – and certain occult agencies and characters. It was certainly the case in the late 19th early 20th century, although this may have been an aberration that has not been repeated. There is no doubt that such characters as Aleister Crowley, Jack Parsons, Theodore Reuss, L. Ron Hubbard, Anton LaVey and centuries earlier Dr John Dee, were known to have worked and co-operated with the intelligence services and the police; but this has also worked the other way round with career soldiers like Col John Alexander and Lt Col Jim Channon. In addition to Alexander and Channon, who, rather than innovate, seem to have exploited, developed and improved on what was already there, at least one other military figure adopted a much more 'hands on' approach regarding the perceived advantages of magic, and that is a former US Army Lt Col named Michael Aquino.

Lt Col Aquino, along with some disaffected members of Anton LaVey's 'Church of Satan' set up his own version of LaVey's creation in 1975, naming it *'The Temple of Set'*; typically the reason why is not obvious, but ostensibly it was because they did not agree with LaVey's methods. Aquino actually went on record to say that 'The Church of Satan' was riddled with corruption, which is in some ways quite surprising considering the very nature of such an organization. Given LaVey's unique philosophy one would think that such a perceived 'crime' might be viewed as a positive trait. Most likely the charges involved money and the abuse of power, and when money is involved, irrespective of which direction the organization takes, then there is bound to be trouble. Once the split was made Aquino went on to incorporate the 'temple' in California as a non-profit church, which is quite appropriate since this established it as a charity, meaning that no taxes were due. This is common practice with all places of worship, charities and other non-profit organizations and was also a ploy used by the late UFO contactee, George Adamski, who, approve of him or not, has carved out an enduring place within the field of Ufology.

Inevitably, membership of the Temple of Set, which offers a total of six degrees from *'Setian'* (first degree) to *'Ipissimus'* (sixth degree), involves the regular payment of money, which allows the initiate to progress through the various degrees of illumination and enlightenment required to permit full spiritual development. Interestingly, the ever-omnipresent Crowley was also an 'Ipissimus', although not of the Temple of Set, the name only signifying one of exalted rank. All groups like this function in similar ways, Scientology, the Rosicrucians (in its AMORC guise) and many more. Unfortunately Col Aquino and his wife, who, incidentally, is said to exist only on egg whites, are reputedly vampires (or as their accusers have it 'vampyres') who regularly consume human blood. It has to be said that pictures of Aquino usually portray him as the archetypal image of Count Dracula with sleek, black hair complete with a widow's peak, and his wife, appropriately named Lilith Sinclair, as the matriarch from the Addams family. Whether they really are genuine vampires is extremely unlikely, but nonetheless the rumors still persist, a ploy that is probably more to do with publicity than anything else.

One additional aspect of the relationship between the Aquinos and the strange atmosphere surrounding the intelligence service/occult axis, which dates back to medieval times, appears yet again in a name, in this case that of Michael Aquino's wife, Lilith, who is a member of the Sinclair clan. This is of course the name of the ancient and influential Scottish family whose antecedents built the legendary and still existing 15th century repository of occult secrets, Rosslyn Chapel. Yes, it might only be sheer happenstance, but if one includes the maiden name of Ian Fleming's mother, St Croix Rose, plus the fact that almost all of these people were known to one another and had similar connections to the occult, then the sheer number of 'coincidences' among such a relatively small number of people seems to stretch credulity just too far. The legends and reputation surrounding Rosslyn Chapel have developed exponentially in the last thirty years or so and are now almost an industry in their own right, but this does not prevent at least some of them from having a footing in reality. Indeed, my own researches into this most enigmatic of buildings, which are described in the book *Rosslyn, Between Two Worlds*, reveal the possibility of a still functioning 'portal' within its walls. What is the connection? The fact that all of these people were drawn together by a shared interest and in two cases carry the names of what have come to be known as 'bloodline' families must surely be much more than coincidental.

St Croix Rose and Sinclair, two powerful and significant names in their own right, are both intimately associated with the secretive orders of the Rosicrucians, the Freemasons, the Knights Templar, and no doubt many more – all organizations steeped in ritual and mystery and all attributed with magical and other occult abilities. The veracity of these claims was and still is a matter for much heated debate, but still the stories and rumors persist, with each claim that the 'truth' had now been revealed and there is no mystery being met by counterclaims saying precisely the opposite. The association that these names have with people and groups actively seeking gnosis concerning hidden truths and the attainment of superhuman abilities through a profound understanding of the nature of reality is almost a given, but why this should be is something else. Perhaps it is the acknowledged destiny of these groups and families to keep the secrets just that, secret, or, as with governmental disinformation campaigns, to ensure that, should any information surface, it is unusable due to adulteration or distortion. As we have seen, attempts by the military to subvert this for their own use is absolutely typical of their mindset and in one way they are to be congratulated on their ingenuity; if it works use it.

Before moving on there is one more character not yet mentioned and that is the late Grady Louis McMurty, once again an officer, this time a major in the US army. Born in 1918, McMurty had an early interest in occultism and joined the Pasadena Agape Lodge of the OTO in June 1941 taking the secret lodge name of *'Hymenaeus Alpha'*, Jack Parsons was also a member of this lodge. McMurty went on to serve as the Caliph from 1969 until his passing in 1985. While serving in Europe during World War II he became friendly with Aleister Crowley who mentored him and was personally initiated into the IX Degree of the OTO by Crowley in his role of 'Baphomet of the XI Degree' and supreme leader of the order. It was also Crowley who originally advised him to take the name Hymenaeus Alpha on the basis that using Greek gematria (a widely employed system of numbers used in divination) came to 777. When Crowley died in 1947 his place as leader of the OTO initially fell to Karl Germer, and upon his death in 1962, due to the fact that he had not appointed a successor, McMurty invoked emergency powers conferred on him by Crowley and assumed the role of Caliph, a role he held until his death in 1985.

Here we have yet another example of the influence of an incredibly influential occult adept and mage, Aleister Crowley, in association with a serving US Army officer. Although arguably only another religion competing with all the rest, it is nonetheless disconcerting that this should be taking place, although there is no evidence that it in any way affected the security within the western sphere of influence. Perhaps it is no more influential than the much more widely acknowledged lodges of Freemasons that dot the world, and although many charges of conspiracy are ranged against them they are relatively low key and what influence they may have is directed locally to the mutual benefit of the brethren.

However, given the background to many of the more extreme examples of societies discussed here, it is likely that they have a much more focused objective. To use individuals in groups like these for the purposes of intelligence gathering and other functions requires a degree of callous cynicism, manipulation and a remarkable degree of pragmatism that frequently marks out those who work in the intelligence agencies the world over. To automatically assume that the users and the used are totally and irretrievably damned must be a given. For the record, my own research indicates that the Freemasons have no connection with the Illuminati or any form of the New World Order; these claims, in my opinion, are founded on speculation and ignorance with no basis in fact.

These then are but a few of those who, by their actions and lifestyle, became equated with the heretics; but this is a description that is not confined solely to magicians. Let us now look at the writers whose prose has terrified countless readers over the years and caused many sleepless nights. We should perhaps begin with one of the best and most influential in the business and that is Howard Philips Lovecraft, creator of both the mighty *'Cthulhu'*, the tentacle headed monstrosity from another dimension and a fictitious book of spells called *The Necronomicon*.

~

Section Two
The Writers

~

Chapter 16
The Writers

H.P. Lovecraft

'And with strange eons even death may die'
The Necronomicon

Howard Philips Lovecraft was born in 1890 in Providence, Rhode Island and apart from a short marriage and a brief time in New York, spent much of his regrettably short life there. During his upbringing, apart from the oppressive attention of his mother, Sarah, who was descended from a long-established Rhode Island family and spent the last two years of her life in a mental institution, there was no obvious connection with anything that would occupy the terrifying nightmare visions of his stories.

The only thing that might provide a tenuous link was his father's rumored membership of 'The Golden Dawn', which, if true, shows just how ubiquitous this organization may have been, given that membership seems to have been restricted to certain levels of society. By a curious act of synchronicity, Lovecraft's father, Winfield Scott Lovecraft, who predeceased his mother by several years, also spent the last days of his life in a mental institution diagnosed with *'paresis'* which is a non-specific term used to bracket a range of neurological ailments. However it has been strongly inferred that in fact he died of syphilis, and cognitive dysfunction is one of the terrible side effects.

As we shall see, the type of work produced by Lovecraft hints a much deeper knowledge influenced, whether consciously or otherwise, by information that did not originate in this reality. For whatever reason, perhaps because Lovecraft himself disliked and distrusted belief in the paranormal, and this appears to include religion, he never subscribed to this idea and S.T. Joshi, who is recognised as one of Lovecraft's main biographers and custodians of his legacy, also rejects this hypothesis. However, it is strongly implied by the previously mentioned magician Kenneth Grant and others, that this was exactly the case. Anyone who has actually read what Lovecraft wrote cannot but fail to be impressed by the descriptions of the literally hellish monsters that exist in the pages of his books, nor have failed to experience a frisson of unease at the mental images they evoke. It has to be said that much of what was conceived and born in Lovecraft's mind came from the wild and alarming dreams that he experienced on a regular basis and this is something that we will return to a little later.

His literary output included such classis of the genre such as, *The Call of Cthulhu* (1926),'*The Case of Charles Dexter Ward* (1927), *The Dunwich Horror* (1928), and *At The Mountains of Madness* (1931), one of the latter two having been made into a successful feature film, *The Dunwich Horror* (Director Daniel Haller) in 1970. The successful and inventive film director, Guillermo Del Toro, recently intended to make another of the books mentioned above, *At The Mountains of Madness,* as a film, but ran into funding difficulties although this project may yet come to fruition. However, the prolific producer and director of horror films, John Carpenter, did direct a similarly titled and effective film, *At The Mouth of Madness* (1995) which featured several Lovecraftian themes involving monstrosities from other dimensions. We should also consider that in reality the work produced by Lovecraft was not strictly supernatural in nature, but rather the stories are more inclined to science fiction in their content. Although it is probably fair to say that they do introduce concepts that were not traditional science fiction in the sense of spaceships and nuts and bolts technology.

Other than the cult that has developed around *The Cthulhu Mythos*, perhaps his best-known creation was the literary device called *'The Necronomicon'*, (also known as *'The Book of Dead Names'*). This book, which is in reality a grimoire, was supposedly assembled many centuries ago by an insane Arab magician, Abdul Alhazred, and is on a par with such works as *'The Grimoire of Pope Honorius'* in its notoriety. The difference is that *The Necronomicon* was a nonexistent work of fiction and the other book was not, although this is not strictly true, because several people, including the authors, L. Sprague De Camp in tandem with George Scithers, have produced versions of *The Necronomicon* for public consumption, basing their actions on the assumption that if there is a ready market for it then why not supply it? Another well-known writer whose output has included several excellent books on occult matters, Colin Wilson, also produced his own version, although he had the good grace to own up to the fact.

The best-known work purporting to be the 'real' *Necronomicon* is a volume known as the *'Simon Necronomicon'*, which is named after its editor who only gives the name, Simon, in the credits. This editor gathered much of the Cthulhu Mythos and combined it with the ancient mythology of Mesopotamia and other strains of mysticism into the finished product. This was actually quite a shrewd move since this location was noted as a hotbed of magic and wizardry from the earliest times. Curiously enough it was also the general area where several biblical prophets were born and perhaps resonates with the hypothesis that magic and religion are not too far apart. The book was first released in 1977 as a limited edition with an appropriate production run of 666 copies and was later reissued by Avon Publishing in 1980 with a greatly increased print run to satisfy a much broader market. What is of great curiosity and interest is why a work of fiction should generate such a furor that a need was felt to actually produce a version – was it only for profit, or was there another reason? Is it the same reason that Lovecraft's work still continues to fascinate and terrify in equal measure? Much as Lovecraft was influenced by the work of Edgar Alan Poe, writers in the horror genre such as Stephen King, Neil Gaiman, Bently Little and doubtless many more, cite Lovecraft as one of their main influences. It should be no surprise then that the beautiful countryside of New England, especially Maine, also features prominently in the work of Steven King.

While the *Necronomicon* has its own avid following, the other – and possibly the most famous of his creations – are the legion of entities that inhabit the pages of his books. They include, *'The Great Old Ones'*, comprising *'Azathoth'*, an entity that seems to roughly equate with the absolute chaos of the singularity that theoretically exists at the bottom of a 'black hole'. Yet another is *'Yog-Sothoth'*, a being that incorporates all of space-time and appears as a shifting swarm of 'iridescent globes' to those who are ill fated enough to actually encounter it. This being is apparently the portal through which the Great Old Ones will eventually re-enter our reality to inflict whatever designs they have upon us.

He also produced such memorable beings as *'Shub-Niggaruth'*, the goat with a thousand young, and *'Hastur the Unspeakable'* also called, *'Him who is not to be named'*, another entity whose malign intentions toward humanity are prevented by measures put into place millennia ago. Might it be blasphemous or even heretical to draw a comparison at this point between the naming of Hastur the Unspeakable and uttering the word of the Tetragrammaton? Both appear to absolutely forbidden to be spoken for fear of the terrible damage they might cause, or is it because they might allow these entities to emerge into our universe? Lovecraft, in a strange resonance with the 'angels' or indescribable 'angles' glimpsed by John Dee, frequently speaks of a place beyond *'the realms of angled space'*.

Why should spoken words hold so much potential earth changing power, what possible latent energy in encapsulated in their structure? A simple question, but the answer it not so straightforward. Since we live in a universe that is founded on vibration we affect what is around to some extent us by generating frequency; yes, there is no perceptible change, but nonetheless theoretically each time a pin drops the Earth vibrates in response to that.

All terrifying prospects, but there is yet one more of Lovecraft's creations that still resonates powerfully in today's society and that is the malign power that is '*Cthulhu*', the semi aquatic entity that traveled from the unknown reaches of the universe in the beginning of time to take refuge here on Earth. Cthulhu, so we are told, currently lies dreaming, entombed in the depths of his city of R'lyeh far below the surface on the seabed of the Pacific Ocean. The accounts of R'lyeh also speak of the incredible angles and unearthly geometry of the buildings that comprise this gigantic sunken citadel. Could this be yet another reference to what was glimpsed by Dee and his assistant Kelley and does this present unexpected evidence for the reality of the presence of non-terrestrial or indeed extra-dimensional entities here on Earth?

Another curious factor in this enigma is the apparent failure of Lovecraft to recognize that he had in effect created an entire cosmology based on his ideas. If he did not see this then his readers certainly did and his influence on his contemporaries in the literary field, such as Clark Ashton Smith and August Derleth, was also quite marked. These two writers of weird fiction, although Lovecraft never actually met them, became good friends and formed what later became known as the 'Lovecraft Circle', communicating through a remarkable volume of letters, so much so that some of Lovecraft's inventions such as 'The Misatonic University' and the town of 'Arkham', both located in Lovecraft's version of New England, appear with their creators full permission in the works of both Smith and Derleth.

Needless to say *The Necronomicon* also appears in their novels and in other places besides, in fact this non-existent work achieved an almost unique place in the realm of the horror genre. Another outlet for this fictional volume appears in Sam Raimi's groundbreaking film, *'The Evil Dead II'*, (1987) where it is referred to as *'The Necronomicon ex Mortis'*, and the act of reading one of its spells aloud opens a swirling portal into another universe and drags the hero of the piece into its ravening maw, unceremoniously depositing him in a demon haunted medieval version of Earth. Fittingly, in the film the book is apparently bound in human skin and has a demonic face deeply embossed on the front cover; it is made quite obvious that the volume is a source of immense and stupefying evil.

Following Lovecraft's death, his memory was enhanced by August Derleth who continued to develop the original ideas created by his friend into a conscious cosmology featuring the *'Outer Gods'* (the Great Old Ones) and their adversaries, the *'Elder Gods'*, who were the saviors of humanity. It was the Elder Gods who battled Cthulhu, Shub-Niggaruth and their ilk and consigned Cthulhu to the submarine fastness of mighty R'lyeh to slumber for all eternity, incapable of harming humanity, or is he? Actually it is not clear whether the Elder Gods were overtly pro-human or not and we merely benefited as a by-product of their animosity towards the Great Old Ones.

As hinted at earlier, were Lovecraft's dreams only the product of his overactive imagination and unearthly dreams, or were they something much more sinister? Is it possible that the unearthly visions were drip-fed into his brain from some unknown outside source, or did he unwittingly draw them to him from the limitless archives of the 'Akashic Records', the storehouse of all human knowledge past, present and future. Did Lovecraft really glimpse the awful horrors that tormented humanity in the distant past, or, as may be more plausible and unlikely as it might seem, did he witness an alternative version of the Earth in some parallel reality where these entities still hold sway.

This leads one to further speculate that his fictitious grimoire, *The Necronomicon,* once actually realized, may be the very vehicle by which these entities seek access to our relatively peaceful universe. Perhaps the money making, so-called 'spoofs' are nothing of the kind. As we already saw with the premise of Chaos Magic and *'fake it till you make it',* perhaps they are designed to spark some reaction in the human psyche to allow the creation of a gateway and perhaps that gateway now exists deep below the ground on the French/Swiss border, the CERN Large Hadron Collider (LHC) that will emulate the conditions when the universe was born. A speculation too far or a possibility? As far as the LHC is concerned we will have to wait and see. Hopefully I am completely wrong, but what if I am not and the nightmares from another plane of existence use the device to slide across the dimensions. Although unlikely, it is not impossible. Perhaps the efforts of the previously mentioned Crowley, Parsons and Hubbard were only partially successful and their 'portal' was too ephemeral to handle the energies required and a much more stable and robust method was required; but as always time will tell.

The Grimoires

Since we have already looked at a fictitious book of spells, *The Necronomicon,* in some detail, perhaps we should turn our attention to another, considerably more lethal and factual work, *The Grimoire of Pope Honorius the Great,* which has already been briefly referred to. This work, which is a French grimoire attributed to Pope Honorius III who died in 1297, has long been regarded as the most evil work on magic ever produced. Its spells and incantations, many of which involve human sacrifice, even outdo those found in *The Key of Solomon, The Sixth and Seventh*

Books of Moses and *The Book of Cyprian*, and invoke such entities as Lucifer and Astaroth, both regarded as the ultimate in evil in the Judeo-Christian tradition.

Once again, we find the concept that in some way the death of a human being will provide the necessary energy either from the blood or life force/soul to permit an entity, whether spiritual or non-terrestrial, passage into this universe. The negative potential in the book caused such mages as Louis Alphonse Constant, better known as *'Eliphas Levi'*, to denounce it as 'an abomination' and 'horrible', 'wicked' and 'profane'. Another more recent occultist, the American born British scholar and former member of The Golden Dawn, A.E Waite (1857-1942) referred to it as 'perhaps the most frankly diabolical of the rituals connected with Black Magic'. Actually Waite, a Roman Catholic, moved in the same social circles as a considerable number of mystical luminaries such as, Madame Helena Petrovna Blavatski (1851-1891) the founder of Theosophy, Annie Besant (1847-1933) a fellow Theosophist, socialist, Marxist and proto women's liberationist, Rudolph Steiner (1861-1925), the esotericist, philosopher and founder of Anthroposophy. Steiner also founded a curious Masonic spin off called, *'The Masonic Order of Memphis and Mizram'* which he led from1906 until approximately 1914. He was also responsible for the concept of biodynamic agriculture.

Waite also knew Wynn Wescott, a high ranking mason, member of The Golden Dawn and co-inventor of the so-called John Dee chess set and the author and occultist Algernon Blackwood, and finally, and perhaps inevitably, the ubiquitous magician, Aleister Crowley. Waite was, in his own right, also a prominent Freemason and was responsible for the translation, publication and popularisation of the works of the previously mentioned French mage, Eliphas Levi. He also eventually became deeply involved in the positive side of mysticism and following the demise of 'The Golden Dawn' formed the *'Fellowship of the Rosy Cross'*, yet another schism of the

Rosicrucians. Unfortunately, Waite was distrusted by both mystics and practitioners of the occult alike; the occultists because he was critical of magical practises and the mystics because of his association with the occult, a prime example of damned if you do and damned if you don't.

Finally, since he is assumed to have compiled and written such a malign tome, what then of Pope Honorius himself? Honorius was born plain Cencio Savelli, and until he joined the priesthood relatively little is known of him, or indeed the Savelli family. However, after this he became treasurer to the Roman Catholic Church, serving under two popes, Pope Clement III (1187-91) and Pope Innocent III (1191-98). In 1197 he was also appointed tutor to the Emperor Frederick II, who himself had been placed under the guardianship of Innocent III. After a brief series of power struggles Honorius was made pope and crowned in August 1216, taking possession of the Lateran in September the same year. One of his other claims to fame, or perhaps infamy, was when he sanctioned the founding of the Dominican order of monks in 1216 and the Franciscans a few years later in 1223.

The Dominicans went on to oversee the murderous excesses and inhuman treatment of many innocents and religious dissenters during the appalling years of the *'Holy Inquisition'*. It may seem strange that people who consider themselves as 'holy' and 'pious', and the Pope is after all 'The Vicar of Christ', should be involved with magic of any kind, let alone so-called 'black magic'. But, the theory goes, since Roman Catholic priests are, with permission, empowered to battle with the supernatural in the form of imps, demons and the other denizens of Hell and send them back from where they came, then, conversely they should be able to summon them too. Perhaps the reasoning went that since the Church was deemed the final arbiter on such matters then it was natural that it should have the deepest understanding of it. While this certainly has some merit it should be remembered that two Dominican monks, Spengler and Kramer, also created a treatise of baleful malice, the *Malleus Malleficorum*, or *Hammer of the Witches*, which was designed as a textbook on both detecting witchcraft and dealing with those adjudged guilty.

The work itself is steeped in a deep-seated and almost obsessive distrust and fear of women, something that, at the time, was endemic in the Catholic Church and to a much lesser extent still is. Once again we are tempted to compare magic and religion for there are many parallels: both involve the invocation of one deity or another, and both are an attempt to bring about a change in reality either by prayer or a spell, and effectively they are quite interchangeable. We, once again, are drawn right back to the context applied to each school of thought; one is deemed holy and therefore 'good' and the other is deemed unholy or Satanic and therefore 'bad'. It might be illuminating to learn what Lovecraft would have made of the question, can good ever be bad and vice versa.

Chapter 17
Robert Ervin Howard

Perhaps we should pause for a second to briefly enter yet another universe, the worlds and heroes created in the fertile mind of Robert Ervin Howard, who almost single-handedly defined a modern genre of writing, one that, while skirting the shrieking horrors of Lovecraft's abominations, also gave a ray of hope in the shape of human beings, albeit courageous and extremely powerful, who were prepared to stand against the dark forces of night and the machinations of sorcerer/kings and fight against their unthinking tyranny. Two of these creations are *Conan the Cimmerian*, better known as *Conan the Barbarian*, and *Solomon Kane*. Conan in particular has become entrenched in the affections of the general public and has of course been portrayed in the cinema to good effect by Arnold Schwarzenegger.

It seems that the inspiration for Conan was actually born of Howard's childhood fascination with the Picts, a barbaric tribe who implacably opposed the Romans in their attempts to colonize Scotland. Their wild, nomadic and harsh lifestyle, plus of course the frequently stark yet beautiful nature of Scotland itself, proved a fertile source of inspiration for him. The creation of Conan and the land of *'Cimmeria'* allegedly occurred in 1932 during one of Howard's frequent trips to Texas when he happened to be in Fredericksburg. During a spell of poor weather he was gazing at a range of hills through a mist of light rain when he realized that this was the ideal terrain for his hero: grim, gloomy and threatening, a hard land for a hard and frequently brutal man. On his return home he worked to put meat on the bones of this idea and filled his 'Hyperborean Age', when Conan walked the Earth, with strange creatures, mysterious races and the by now inevitable magic.

His other creation, Solomon Kane, was a 17th century English Puritan who roamed the far corners of his world seeking out and destroying evil in all its forms. He did this using a mixture of fervent religiosity, guile and brute force, backed by a rapier, a dagger and two flintlock pistols. In addition to these implements he carried a mysterious staff given to him by an African shaman, which naturally was no ordinary length of wood. This was none other than the fabled *'Staff of Solomon'*, an artifact almost as old as time, which was once in the care of an ancient order of priests devoted to good. The staff, which was pointed at one end with a cat's head adorning the other, had been used to slay vampires and was possessed of great intrinsic spiritual energy which Kane could harness against his more obstinate foes.

As befits his general demeanor, Kane is described as dressed completely in black with a pale complexion and hard, cold, glittering eyes. He was also given to wearing a large, slouched, wide brimmed hat tipped slightly over one eye. This added atmospheric detail from Howard's imagination may have been hijacked by a wrestler called 'The Undertaker' to add gravitas to the almost supernatural image he tries to project, in fact his entire appearance seem to echo that of Kane. It has been speculated in some quarters that Kane represented a facet of Howard's views on religion, particularly given the fire and brimstone nature of some of Kane's sermons given in the course of the various tales. At the time of writing, probably cashing in on the current popularity of heroic comic book and pulp fiction characters, a film is being made of his exploits.

Not surprisingly, Howard became an intimate of Lovecraft and joined The Lovecraft Circle, the literary self-help group of like-minded authors who actively shared ideas and concepts and encouraged one another in their efforts. Were these actions altruistic or was there another function? The question must be asked if each member of this group contributed some energy to Lovecraft, the man at its core, and empowered him in his work as he revealed the nightmare worlds of his creations. Might Lovecraft have reposed there like a kind of 'psychic vampire' relying on the input from his associates to give him the strength that his poor health could not?

Whatever the truth or otherwise of this notion, Howard had his own demons to deal with in the shape of bouts of severe depression that descended on him throughout his life. He partly attributed the condition to his Irish ancestry and partly to the sneers of derision he endured from his neighbors who considered his choice of profession as an author to be somehow demeaning. They considered that he should have taken a 'proper job' as a tradesman of some kind, and given Howard's naturally shy and diffident personality, this might have been the best choice. He took his own life in 1936 after a particularly severe bout of depression.

Prior to this sad event he told his friends that had it not been for the poor health of his mother, who was almost totally bedridden with tuberculosis, he would have taken his life. His death at thirty years of age undoubtedly robbed an eager and rapidly expanding fan base of further adventures devoted to his heroic and magical creations and probably those of several new ones. Howard's notion that his condition may have had its roots in his ancestry is not new and may reflect the tendency for those of Celtic extraction to have an almost instinctive attraction for spiritual matters. This manifests in the numbers of seers and 'wise women' and others who exhibit the so-called 'second sight' and proliferate in traditional Celtic cultures.

Chapter 18
Breaking the Circle

There is one more possibility to examine here, was Howard's ultimate demise caused by his membership of The Lovecraft Circle? Did it slowly drag down the few defenses that he still possessed until he had nothing left, and did the unearthly subjects he regularly dealt with act as the final catalyst causing him to lose the very will to live? Sadly we will never know because all the members of this group are now dead, and although there are still a few writers who explore the genre, there will never be another like it. The one thing that still remains unsaid is this: did this group of like-minded authors unwittingly facilitate in a process begun much earlier by Aleister Crowley at Boleskine House on the banks of Loch Ness? Is it possible that Jack Parsons and L Ron Hubbard brought this unholy process to fruition in 1947 when they attempted the arcane rituals of the *Babalon Working*, a magickal procedure designed to open a portal into another dimension? Was this a weird fusion of magic and literature planned eons ago by unknown intelligences to bring their dominion to our reality? Perhaps the events since them speak for themselves, but not in any huge planetary conflagration.

What we have seen to date are a series of relatively small wars in various areas of the planet, nothing too big, but still a drain on resources and a steady release of hatred and negativity. Other sources of hatred are the many examples of religious intolerance that find expression in the sheer volume of terrorist outrages perpetrated worldwide in a attempt to coerce the free world into a unified belief. We have seen society crumble slowly into a morass of haves and have-nots, the cynical and deliberate creation of an underclass that has become totally dependent of welfare benefits as a way of life, and this had become acceptable in an atmosphere where any manner of dissent or resistance is howled down by the forces of political correctness. This group includes those who insist upon and deify the democratic process yet deny those who espouse alternative views their right to expression.

Sheltering under the politically correct liberal umbrella are other groups committed to anarchy in society and the destruction of law and order, intending to replace it with an unworkable utopia. To make one's voice heard and speak out against this foolish dependent culture is to be branded as intolerant, and to openly criticize appalling lifestyle choices even more so. This is how it may begin as society slowly implodes and collapses, ripe for a takeover by those who desire to control it. As if this was not bad enough, the really worrying part is that these vested interests may not even be human.

This was strongly hinted at during a lengthy series of séances and psychic experiments facilitated by Mr Robin Foy and other members of '*The New Spiritual Science Foundation*' and conducted during the 1990's by 'The Scole Group' in the village of Scole in the county of Norfolk, England. These unique experiments were independently refereed by members of such respected organizations as the Society of Psychical Research (SPR) and some of the findings were literally staggering in their implications. In the course of the project a number of images were taken using specially arranged video and 35mm film cameras; and these pictures, which were taken in complete darkness with the recording devices completely isolated and enclosed, revealed a variety of objects including pyramidal shapes and what looked like planets. In addition to these were many images of color swirls and what looked like faces in the process of forming, but there was one single frame that was truly astonishing. This single frame of videotape clearly depicted an entity that the team named 'blue' on account of the faint blue color wash associated with the image; in fact the picture shows the head, complete with large, slanted, black eyes, of what in any other context would be called a 'grey', the ubiquitous entity normally associated with sightings of UFO's their occupants. I will continue to use the description, 'grey' since it is already familiar and is immediately associated with non-human and extraterrestrial beings.

During a series of experiments, which spanned several years, The Scole Group had been apparently been willingly assisted by a number of discarnate entities that they called, *'The Spirit Team'*. This group of 'spirit beings' consisted of a wide range of entities from throughout history, the oldest dating from the 13th century up to the present. Unfortunately, as is often the way with such projects, during the course of the experiment one of the beings calling itself 'Manu' was asked several potentially vital questions and although having much to say actually imparted little of any value. This has been my own experience in such circumstances, although ostensibly pleasant and helpful, any answers supplied by such beings tend to be vague and oblique.

In spite of this, it was through this unlikely agency that the group learned that these 'grays' were in fact not extraterrestrial, but originated from other dimensions and realities that existed in parallel with our own. This new interpretation is one that might make sense of some of the attributes associated with both the entities and their means of transport. It also might cause us to rethink how we view what happens to consciousness after the death of our physical bodies. The Spirit Team also imparted the much more worrying information that in addition to the ubiquitous grays there were other entities infinitely more dangerous to humanity; in fact, if they could, they would destroy us with no compunction whatsoever. They lurk in the shadow realities eyeing us with loathing and an all consuming jealousy.

The reason for this is apparently because in our current stage of development we are flesh and blood and experience deep feelings and emotions and this is something they cannot do; therefore they hate us with an unthinking and implacable passion. Perhaps they are the so-called *'Shadow People'*, alleged entities we will return to in depth in the fourth section of this book.

This also suggests the possibility that, rather than some parallel if inimical civilization, they may even figure as part of our own evolutionary process, although at which juncture it is difficult to say. The implication drawn from the Spirit Team was that these beings are the demons and devils that occasionally break the through the walls of reality by any means possible to torment and prey upon us. This leads us to wonder if it is to these beings that Lovecraft and his associates alluded in their books and short stories, all of them in thrall to the vicarious pleasures and seductive promises entrained in the powerful emanations from these savage entities trapped in their hidden dimensions?

It also causes one to speculate that it was a gateway or portal to permit their entry to our reality that Crowley, Parsons and Hubbard strove to create in order to achieve their own ends, and Lovecraft instinctively presented as elaborate word pictures connected to our deepest thoughts, any pleasure that they could imagine and many that they could not – deep, dark, wild and limitless. Strange, savage yet strangely beautiful in their stark imagery do they still linger in the mind's eye like avatars and archetypes imprinted in our DNA as long suppressed race memories? This may be the reason why some of us have an instinctive aversion to many reptiles, fish and insects physically much smaller than us. Consider our illogical adverse reaction to spiders, reptiles and many of the more extreme species of deep-sea fish. Some of this is of course common sense, especially when encountering one of the many poisonous species of snakes etc, but the unthinking fear extends to include all snakes and of course spiders almost irrespective of size. We fear and are repulsed by their very appearance, their sheer unpredictability and the jerky, sparky, predatory thought processes that govern their very existence.

Magic and science, incompatible or inseparable? From what we have seen in this section of the book it becomes clear that the two disciplines are more closely allied than it might first appear. The main stumbling block to integration is the intolerance of the scientific community, particularly the one that espouses the mechanistic, Newtonian view of the world. To have an effect one must first have a measurable cause, and as we have seen this is not necessarily true; but as the still almost arcane branch of science called Quantum Physics appears to demonstrate, even a wish can produce a solid outcome. All that is required is a change of paradigm; in other words, keep an open mind and such a viewpoint may be required when reading the next section of this book. How did the human race become established on the face of the Earth?

~

Section Three

The Great Enigma

~

Chapter 19
ET's and Intelligent Design

"I think we're property. I should say that we belong to something: that once upon a time this Earth was no-man's-land, that other worlds explored and colonized here and fought amongst themselves for possession, but that now it's owned by something. That something owns this Earth – all others warned off".
Charles Hoy Fort, visionary and anomalist (1874 – 1932)

There is a long-standing and fierce debate between those, *'The Creationists'*, who attribute our existence on planet Earth to an invisible entity called Almighty God and those, *'The Evolutionists'*, who prefer to believe that we are the product of circumstance, a random collection of chemicals that somehow eventually coalesced into a single-celled amoeba, an amoeba that possessed one unique and absolutely crucial feature, it contained the constituents and blueprints of the DNA molecule. This is the same molecule that through its coding evolved in myriad ways to end up as the human race and everything else on the face of the planet. Every plant, every insect and every animal share that common link, the DNA molecule in one form or another. All display remarkable similarities, but it is the few percentage points of difference that shape the final product. Sheer chance or divine intervention, is that the only choice? Perhaps not, so let's look at the options.

There is yet another variant on these conventions and that is a concept called *'Intelligent Design'* (ID); in other words, the sheer complexity involved in the organisms that cover the planet cannot have appeared through evolution and natural selection and, accordingly, must have had considerable outside assistance. This is a concept eagerly debunked by the Evolutionist lobby as Creationism by the back door, but it is not. There is nothing set in stone to say that the designer was some divine entity existing outside space and time that literally wished reality into being by fiat, in other words a Creator God. The 'missing link' is the possibility that, yes, life on the Earth was indeed put here by an outside source, but not by any mystical or supernatural entity; instead this may have been introduced by the hotly debated agency of an enigmatic non-terrestrial intelligence. It also raises the significant point that terrestrial DNA may not be the sole design parameter for what we define as plant or animal life, perhaps for life on this planet, but not everywhere, and we shall consider that too. Incidentally, while ET intervention is a proposition that for different reasons both the Evolutionists and the Creationists camps reject out of hand, neither does it do either school of thought any credit to arrogantly assume that all life must conform to our conceptions and norms.

The words attributed to the late Charles Fort that open this section, and incidentally a view shared by William Bramley the influential author of the *'The Gods of Eden'*, are of particular import to the study of the paranormal in all its diverse forms, in particular to those who choose to take the view that we are not alone in the universe and our home here on Earth was chosen for us. Within the frequently paranoid and, sadly, occasionally delusional world of UFO's, there are, like it or not, several splinter groups including, *'Ufologists'*, *'Saucerians'* plus a strange amalgam of quasi-religious cults. These latter groups, who I shall call the *'True Believers'*, attribute the non-human entities that presumably pilot the craft with the abilities of a Creator God. Conversely, as we shall also soon discover, there are fundamentalist evangelical Christian groups who are equally certain that these craft and their occupants are the agents of Satanic forces.

Of the other two groups the Ufologists are perhaps the more sober in the respect that they actively seek answers to the enigma, while the Saucerians unquestioningly accept that we have been, and continue to be, visited by benevolent, non-terrestrial entities who traverse the voids of space in craft of various designs, but normally circular and occasionally triangular in shape. However, although giving them a considerable amount of respect bordering on adulation, they stop short of actual worship. The third group, the 'True Believers', are something else entirely and seem to have developed from within the ranks of the Saucerians. They appear to have experienced some sort of spiritual vacuum, and rather like believers in search of a belief they sought to fill it with something greater than themselves and their epiphany came with the saucers.

The concept behind the True Believers is quite seductive; they need the comfort of knowing that there is something greater than the human race, but would prefer to ascribe it to space-farers rather that to a God; it is a belief that deserves at least some attention and perhaps the best place to begin is with their outlook. It is at this point that the subject of UFO's teeters on the cusp of becoming a religion that, incidentally, is refuted by fundamentalist Christians who, as previously mentioned define the UFO's, and especially their presumed occupants, as Satanic in origin. This is based on the grounds that the bible does not specifically mention them other than to talk about, 'Satan-Prince of the Power of the Air, Lord of those that Fly'. This is also sometimes quoted as, 'The Antichrist will honor Satan, called Baal, Lord of Fortresses, Lord of High Places, Lord of those who fly quickly in the high places, Prince of the Power of The Air', all definitions that apply to the denizens of Hell. Both of these interpretations infer that Satan must be the force behind the craft (and their occupants) that fly in the high places (presumably outer space and/or Earth's atmosphere). The Book of Daniel mentions, '...He shall honor the God of Fortresses and he shall honor a God whom his fathers (the Jews) did not know'. This last sentence implies that this God must by definition be unknown and therefore 'alien'.

What we read here is a remarkably literal, narrow and short-sighted definition since the bible does not mention many things including organ transplants, aircraft, electricity, radio and television etc or, incidentally, manned space flight. These developments, including manned space flight originating here on Earth, have to my knowledge not yet been deemed Satanic, although small sects like the Mennonites and the Amish do tend to reject all forms of technology on principle, preferring to rely on almost medieval technology. Having said that, no doubt if one looked hard enough one could probably find some scrap of text that could taken out of its context and made to fit whatever point one wished to make. These extreme beliefs also find expression in the ideas of the Jehovah's Witnesses and the Christian Scientists (CS) who, respectively, eschew blood transfusions and medical procedures. It is a situation that has directly lead to the deaths of many of the adherents of these faiths; evidently their faith was not sufficiently strong to overcome the biological short-comings of their bodies.

The Christian Scientists do have members who, despite having no medical qualifications, style themselves as 'doctors' and 'nurses' and wield their beliefs instead of medicine with varying degrees of success. Neither group normally uses psychic healers, which, logically, should be acceptable since they frequently rely on prayer and religious observance to promote cures. This is exactly the same provenance claimed by other healers who channel 'divine energy' to bring about their treatments. It may be that the CS 'doctors' bring about their dubious cures through the inadvertent exploitation of psychosomatic conditions, in other words the 'patients' cure themselves through mind over matter, something that we are all capable of doing and it is possible that the psychics are doing much the same thing. As our knowledge of molecular biology increases and our technology develops so that we can look ever deeper into the construction of the building blocks of life, it becomes clear that fundamentally we are electrochemical machines. It follows then that at some point in the future we may be able to recreate a living human being entirely from suitably prepared chemical compounds and catalysts without recourse to any human intermediary. This, according to tradition, is absolute anathema and by orthodoxy the realm of God alone, so out of respect (and fear) we should leave well alone.

Undoubtedly, should the expertise and technical ability ever develop to a point where it becomes possible, it is certain that it would be attempted, although for obvious reasons it would have to be in the strictest secrecy, somewhere in the infamous world of 'black projects' that acts as a screen for some truly amazing and possibly nightmarish technology. To refer to these creations as 'synthetic' or 'artificial' – and make no mistake about it, this description will be used, much as the media christened genetically modified cereals and grains as *'Frankenstein foods'* – is disingenuous, because it matters not whether they came from a womb or a Petri-dish, they are still human beings. The real point of interest comes from how they would interact socially and develop in their own right as beings if they had no characteristics inherited from parents, in effect a zero genetic legacy. Of course, depending on the state of the technology that created them, perhaps this could be built into the DNA matrix of their being, or even imprinted on their brains at a later stage. The only possible downside comes from the purpose for which this technology might be used; if science can create a viable human being, could this also open the door to a race of super beings, the forerunners of the much speculated upon 'supersoldiers'?

Chapter 20
The Religionists

As already mentioned, the Creationists and organized religion would strive tooth and nail to prevent such experiments from ever taking place and would be vociferous in their objections. Examples of this reaction have already been seen in the fundamentalist movements in the USA where workers in abortion and family planning clinics have been harassed and even killed by pro-life activists. This raises another interesting point, in a curious parallel with embryos, would a human being created entirely by science have a soul? I hasten to add that I am not promoting any esoteric theological debate here, but using the concept of 'soul' to illustrate how religion might view the spiritual status of a being not directly born of human beings. If such a being lived a full lifespan and died, would their consciousness also pass to the afterlife?

Indeed, would such a being even have the prospect of an afterlife? It might be instructive to see how organized religion responds to such questions, because logically if the being is by all measurable parameters human, which it must be irrespective of where it came from, then it must also possess a 'soul'. The same should apply to its 'spirit', since spirit is synonymous with 'life essence' or consciousness, and it is this that transcends death to pass to the next stage of existence. The answers to these questions would surely give a valuable insight into how religion regards the nature and validity of the soul/spirit. It would also be fascinating to see how such a being would develop in the world, assuming of course that he/she was allowed to integrate fully into society and perhaps even marry and have offspring of their own. However, as far as we are concerned, all of this is speculation and something for future generations to decide. But on the other hand what if this technology was far from new, what if it brought the human race into existence? What if this was something that was completely erased from our memories at every possible level, cellular, racial and genetic?

Perhaps we should reflect on the proposition of many Creationists who, perversely, insist that the Earth is less than 10,000 years old. Bishop Ussher came to a similar conclusion centuries ago when he deduced from his calculations based on scripture that the Earth was created fully-fledged and inhabited in 4004BC. This pious and sincerely held belief became accepted wisdom for a time and was corroborated by such luminaries as the founder of Protestantism, the German monk Martin Luther (1483-1546) and the astronomer, Johannes Kepler (1571-1630), whose researches revealed the laws of planetary motion. Kepler also developed convex eyepieces for telescopes and was a noted mathematician and astrologer, because at that time astronomy and astrology were viewed as complimentary subjects.

While astrology is currently viewed as sheer hokum by conventional science, nevertheless it has revealed some astonishing insights into shared personality traits among historical figures born under specific seasonal star charts. One tentative explanation put forward for this phenomenon relates to the possible effects of electromagnetic fields caused by the alignment of celestial bodies, particularly the sun, throughout the year on unborn foetuses. All of these characters were highly intelligent men, all were absolutely sincere, and all were absolutely wrong. The problem, sadly, is that the Bible is not a reliable source to use for the accurate timing or veracity of historical events. There have been too many interested parties and vested interests involved in its various translations, each with their own axe to grind. It has often been said that men wrote the Bible, not God, and that is very true.

Chapter 21
Life as we Know It?

If we are the sole creation of a supreme being and one considers what is involved in this, surely one can speculate on why should God go to all that trouble? Taken to the level of a machine, the human body, especially the brain, is a truly astonishing piece of engineering that almost beggars belief in its complexity and subtlety. Why would any sentient entity, assuming that God is sentient in any meaningful sense, go to the bother of designing a device like a human brain with its capability for infinite shades of nuance, intelligence, flexibility and decision making? This organic device is part and parcel of a self-replicating species and perhaps its main redeeming feature is that it is capable of learning and more importantly is capable of original thought; and it is this single feature that elevates it far beyond the range of any computer irrespective of how 'smart' it is – so far! It is also reasonable to ask whether a God would or should expect its creations to worship and praise it and severely punish those that did not, irrespective of whether or not they had ever heard of it.

If it created us then, in an echo of the previously mentioned 'Who Mourns for Adonis' why not 'program in' unquestioning belief to avoid the necessity of punishment and guarantee its divinity? But surely the very desire to be worshipped reflects badly on the vain, peevish, selfish and shallow nature of such a being. It is very likely that the God-based version of creation developed through the inability of ancient philosophers, chroniclers and prophets to understand the nature of what they saw. Lacking the knowledge and technology, and probably influenced to some extent by fear, they described the process by the only method that made perfect sense to them: it had to have come via a supreme being, God. There was nothing wrong with their logic or reasoning, but it was limited by their lack of understanding of the world or the cosmos. Now, however, we are in a much different position to both challenges, and can at least attempt to prove the alternatives.

If, then, we are not the product of a God, did we develop naturally and by accident or was it the result of some external force? One strain of True Believers such as *'The Raelians'* are sure this is the case and still prepare for the return of 'the creators' and they revere their founder, Rael, a former racing driver, as a semi-divine intermediary. This, unfortunately, is a very human failing and has appeared many times in a variety of UFO based cults such as the *'Aetherius Society'* who virtually deified their founder, ex-taxi driver, 'Dr' George King. 'Dr' King claimed to act as a channel for the *'Cosmic Masters'* whose numbers allegedly included Jesus, Buddha, Krishna and a number of other diverse religious icons and prophets.

Even although their founder is long dead, the society still exists and is active in several countries. Another example, but to a slightly lesser degree, was 'Dr', sometimes 'Professor', George Adamski, an acknowledged publicity seeker and alleged UFO 'contactee' who, like the aforementioned Rael, attained an almost Messiah-like status among his devotees. Strangely enough, it once again seems to be almost *de rigueur* that people who are elevated to figureheads within these slightly eccentric groups adopt titles such as 'doctor' or 'professor' and it is likely that it is for the same reasons as self styled magicians. Sects and cults aside, is this the answer, or is there another alternative, one that mediates between the extremes and produces an acceptable solution? The fundamental question is this: are we the result of an extraterrestrial chemistry experiment?

The Proposition

The answer is very probably yes, and in my opinion this came about in one of two ways. Both are distinct possibilities and both, in the main, fall within the conventions of accepted science. But both have their unique problems; consider this. According to a theory developed by Dr. William Hartman, an American astronomer and 'planetary scientist', when the Earth gradually formed approximately five billion years ago, it evolved along with the rest of the planets orbiting our Sun, from an accretion of dust, rock and other elements into a super-hot ball of magma, and as it cooled it spewed out clouds of vapour and slowly became a habitable dwelling place. In the course of the cooling down period some of the ejected gases were in the form of water vapor that gradually condensed and over the aeons filled the vast gullies and trenches covering the surface to comprise the seas and oceans.

This is all well and good until one considers that there is one major factor against this: what we recognize as the Earth's surface is not the original one; in fact what there is of the original surface takes the form of relatively few, small, very hardwearing zircon crystals embedded in the rocks of a range of hills in Western Australia. However, at a point approximately five hundred million years after the planet first formed, there was a catastrophic encounter, a collision in fact, with another cosmic body named *'Theia'*, another planet believed to have orbited our sun just after the solar system came into being. This small planet, which was approximately the size of Mars, grazed the surface of the Earth dislodging a gigantic mass of debris that initially formed a belt around the Earth then eventually coalesced into our moon. Or, alternatively, the moon may be what remains of the object that crashed into our planet. If the collision did actually take place then it is logical to assume that the moon as it is now must contain debris and matter from both the Earth and Theia and conversely the Earth must contain some of the alien debris as well. As far as our moon is concerned, samples gathered from its surface by various expeditions, both manned and unmanned, have revealed the presence of rocks, and especially dust, that is considerably older than the Earth. This is a something that will also be looked at later as part of a wider issue and in a slightly different context.

The cataclysm, which ushered in the appropriately named '*Hadean Age*', about which very little is known, caused the planet to melt back down to its core and begin the process of solidifying once again. It also virtually guarantees that life only came into existence at some point after the earth was five hundred million years old. What this means is that the present surface of the Earth is nothing like the original and still required that water be produced to fill depressions in the reformed outer shell. All of the original condensate would have vanished in the searing conflagration of the collision and that would have to be replaced from somewhere; the simple axiom as far as we are concerned is, no water, no life. It is for this reason that we eagerly search for signs of water in any form in other planets in our solar system and elsewhere.

Current thinking suggests that the majority of the water here on Earth came from another outside source, and that is from comets that are mostly formed of ice and rock. In fact comets have sometimes been called, 'dirty snowballs'. The appearance of abundant water may have occurred during what is called the '*Late Heavy Bombardment*', when, as the name suggests, the planet was pummeled over a considerable time by wandering lumps of cosmic debris. Although there is no definitive proof that this is what actually occurred, it is the most recent best guess. This is turn leads to the assumption that there must have been a solid and impermeable base to receive and hold the arriving water otherwise it would have instantly 'flashed off' as superheated steam from the bubbling magma. Convention insists that from these unpromising and hostile beginnings life began: simple chemicals gradually mixed into the more complex substances necessary to produce life and this is something we will return to.

Before progressing any further we should perhaps consider one of the Bible's best-known stories, and that is the story of the 'Great Flood', which, once again, is often taken literally by Christian fundamentalists. According to the Bible, it is implied that the entire planet was immersed in a deluge that lasted forty days and forty nights and caused horrendous flooding that resulted in the death of all humanity and all animal life except for Noah and his family and of course two each of every animal and insect species on Earth. Once the rain stopped and the water abated, the Ark was grounded on Mt Ararat where, presumably, the human race re-established itself along with every other species. Quite apart from the logistics involved in building the vessel and stocking it with male and female examples of every animal and insect, (the fish would, quite naturally, have been in their element anyway), there is the puzzle of the water; where did it all come from?

At present, although most of the Earth's surface is covered in water, there is insufficient to totally inundate the planet. So The Flood as described in the Bible simply cannot have happened on the scale suggested, there is simply not enough free water – perhaps some localized inundation, a tsunami, but nothing on a global scale, not even close. The only way in which this might have occurred would be if all the polar ice caps had melted, and there is no evidence for this; even then, although water levels would have risen appreciably, there would still not have been enough to completely inundate all the land surfaces. The accounts of what was aboard the Ark in in terms of the sheer diversity of animals, and the logistics of feeding them, have to be viewed with great care; they are an allegory not facts. If Noah did suffer a localized flood and attempted to save his family and livestock in a boat, then this is just about acceptable; but the rest is, in my opinion, a fantasy invented by chroniclers who came much later to make sense of the legend and demonstrate the powers of their God.

Charles Darwin, a pivotal figure in biological and scientific academia, who originally propounded the concept of evolution and natural selection, depicted this process as occurring in some sort of idyllic 'warm pond', when nothing could be further from the truth. If the building blocks of life did actually combine in some notional 'warm pond', it was almost certainly more akin to the conditions found adjacent to the scalding hot volcanic vents on the ocean floor where highly specialized types of life exist. In other words, according to the tenets of evolution, we emerged from a boiling, salty, inhospitable environment and over millions of years gradually became, for good or ill, what we are. Again this has its inherent problems: if DNA molecules developed then they required proteins and the designs for these proteins are encoded in the DNA – a classic 'chicken and egg' scenario.

Before moving to the next chapter, let's return briefly to the previously mentioned Dr William Hartman. According to Dr Hartman, the newly formed moon was very much closer to the Earth, a little over 15,000 miles away in fact, and the gravitational pull was very much greater than it is now resulting is powerful tides and currents in the seas. The necessary minerals and chemicals were scoured from the walls and banks of the channels and rivers, cut into the land masses by the action of the seas and taken into the relative calm of these deep waters to mix and mature. Although this is another variant on how the constituent chemicals mixed, it still fails to explain what may be an insoluble puzzle: at which point do 'dead' chemicals become 'alive'? Is this what is meant by the 'spark of life'? Is this the very breath of God infusing existence into what is by all measurable parameters devoid of life? Or are these descriptions merely an attempt to explain and rationalize what our ancestors had no answer to? It is to this hypothetical 'spark of life' that we turn our attention next.

Chapter 22
The Millar-Urey Experiment

In 1953 a series of laboratory experiments were conducted at the University of Chicago by Stanley Miller and Harold Urey in an attempt to recreate the conditions thought to be prevalent when life first appeared on the Earth. This also was the birth of a scientific discipline called *'prebiotic chemistry'* and the process became known as *'The Miller-Urey Experiment'*. The concept was designed to test a hypothesis first promoted by Haldane and Oparin who suggested that, given the right conditions, inorganic components on the early Earth could be metamorphosized into organic compounds.

The two researchers built an apparatus resembling two glass spheres, each about the size of a soccer ball located one on top of the other and connected using tubes with electrodes set into the top flask. The bottom sphere was half filled with a mix of water, methane, ammonia and hydrogen, all assumed to have been present during the formation of the planet, and heat was applied. As steam was produced through evaporation, it was introduced into the top flask where the electrodes were located and electrical discharges were produced within the top flask to simulate lightning in the hope that chemical compounds would appear. The condensate in the top flask then ran back into the bottom in a continuous process. Unfortunately the experiments, although not entirely successful, did, after a week of continuous operation, produce a small amount of the amino acids necessary to manufacture proteins. Certain sugars and some of the other components of nucleic acids were also produced.

The work started by Millar and Urey has continued intermittently ever since, and as recently as 2008 eleven vials left from the original experiment were re-evaluated by another team of scientists using much more effective and sensitive measuring equipment. They were able to identify additional organic molecules not previous noted by Millar and Urey and confirmed that the best results came from the original attempt to recreate 'volcano like' conditions. In spite of the lack of complete success it still does not mean that it cannot be done. Significantly, the hypothesis of the 'warm pool' put forward by Darwin may have been infinitely bigger than he might originally have envisioned. Another experiment conducted in 2006 indicated that a dense organic haze, which contained various concentrations of methane and carbon dioxide, might have existed over much of the very early Earth.

These microscopic organic molecules would have dispersed and proliferated naturally all over the surface of the planet bringing with them the necessary building blocks by means of convection currents, winds and other forces. It is an astonishing mental image, the entire planet completely enveloped in a mantle of fog containing the seeds of life itself, like a gigantic biochemistry set. The experiments first promoted in 1953 still continue, but there are, however, some serious questions being put forward concerning where we as a race go from here. Do we continue to evolve, or since the creation of life has apparently not been successfully replicated either naturally or artificially, has our evolution as a species now effectively ceased?

The answer to this is at best unclear, which, in turn, since the original creation of the human race as envisioned by scripture although convenient is extremely unlikely, invites another and much more viable solution. However it is not one that sits comfortably with any paradigm so far mentioned; it is called '*Panspermia*'. Before considering this, perhaps we should take a look at Darwin and what his far-reaching and radical discoveries implied. Incidentally, in spite of the limited success of the experiments from 1953 onwards, the method by which chemicals become 'alive' has still not been discovered, or so we are told; yet it happens quite naturally the world over hundreds of times each second when children are conceived. However that analogy is not quite accurate since the sperm and egg are both 'alive', but require to be merged with one another to allow life to commence. Before leaving what was attempted in the Millar-Urey experiment, we should consider what was in many ways its direct predecessor and that was the astonishing work carried out by Andrew Crosse in 1837. It was in this year that Crosse allegedly succeeded in using the then novel medium of electrical power to create a type of life, in this case an entirely new species of insect.

Chapter 23
The Crosse Experiments

A truly fascinating precursor to the experiments made famous by Millar and Urey was the work carried out by a man who must surely have been one of the last of the English 'gentleman scientists'. He was a dilettante in the truest and best sense of the word and his name was Andrew Crosse, (1784-1855). In a classic example of synchronicity, Crosse carried out a series of experiments using electricity, although his original purpose was quite different. He was born to a wealthy land owning family and was regarded as something of a prodigy having managed to learn Greek by the age of eight. On reaching the age of nine he was sent for further schooling to the seaport of Bristol where he became fascinated by the new science of electricity, the possibilities of which later became an obsession with him.

When his mother died in 1805 he inherited a considerable sum of money, more than enough to support him, and also the isolated family seat of Fyne Court mansion house located in the Quantock Hills of Somerset, England. The isolation of his home was ideally suited to his experimentation, and in order to tap into the natural power of lightning, he laid out a network of copper cables, over a mile in length that radiated from his laboratory like the threads of a shining web. Naturally, the largely uneducated locals grew to distrust and eventually fear him and the sight of lightning strikes from the thunderstorms that occasionally swirled and roiled around the hills arcing along the network of cables, terrified them. It has to be said that anyone, especially then, who tried to use the intermittent raw energy of lightning as a source of power was, from the point of view of safety, on very thin ice indeed, and it can only be due to luck that he was not killed. It is also not at all clear how he regulated the short lived burst of voltage created by the lightning to a usable level since he must have been carrying out these experiments largely by guesswork. It may have been that he used it to charge capacitors for a later and slower discharge, but once again this is not made obvious.

In the course of his experiments, which were originally intended to produce artificial minerals from saturated solutions, he made another and potentially explosive discovery. His apparatus, which comprised a cloth siphon causing a drip feed of the sample liquid from a top container onto a piece of porous red oxide which was kept electrified in a lower container, was under constant close observation by means of a magnifying glass to detect signs of spontaneous crystal growth. After fourteen days there appeared what he described as small whitish 'excrescences' and on the eighteenth day they enlarged slightly and produced seven to eight filaments. On the twenty-sixth day each of the 'excrescences' resembled tiny insects and moved their 'legs'. A few days later they detached themselves and moved around independently. Naturally Crosse was astonished and repeated the experiment with identical results.

Crosse named the insects *'acari'* and once again carried out the experiments using a range of materials, and still with the same results. Eventually he wrote up the experiments in meticulous detail and sent the documentation to the Electrical Society in London, where, after initial skepticism, one Mr. W.H Weeks, a well known scientist, was commissioned to replicate the Crosse experiments. Weeks employed even more stringent controls, including sterilization of all the equipment, but in spite of this succeeded in producing near identical results and the tiny creatures were called *'Acarus Crossi'* in honor of their discoverer/creator. Quite naturally the religious authorities were outraged at this supposed blasphemy and the local clergyman, a

Rev Philip Smith, after suitably stirring up the locals, actually exorcised Crosse's estate. The story/mythology surrounding this discovery goes on to insist that even today no scientist is willing to attempt this remarkable experiment and one might justifiably ask why? What is there to fear?

So goes the tale, which supplies more questions than answers; it has been suggested that the small mites were already present as eggs in the atmosphere or on the samples used by both experimenters. Did Crosse perhaps bribe Weeks into corroborating his claims? He certainly had the money. Why would modern science not follow up these experiments, which would surely prove whether there was some basis in fact for the claims made by Crosse and Weeks? It cannot be due to fear of religious wrath, for if it were proved correct then surely this would be a major discovery? One thing that does strike a sympathetic chord are the conditions (extremely caustic) in which these 'acari' appeared – they developed in a hostile environment analogous to the briny cauldrons that spawned our own templates for life.

The story of Crosse and his experiments carry more than a little of the feel of the story of Frankenstein: the purpose was the same, the details are all there even down to the superstitious reactions of the villagers surrounding his estates. It also resonates strongly with the use of lightning as Mary Shelley's vision for the motivating power behind Baron Victor Frankenstein's experiments. Is it possible that she knew of what Crosse did and used it as a template for her own creation? It is almost impossible to separate the gothic images created by the cinema with what went on at Fyne Court. But the doubt still persists in spite of claims to the contrary. Were these insects actually created or is this just one more semi-scientific hoax perpetrated on a gullible society and carried on into modern times by the theorists convinced that we are manipulated by 'them', the 'Illuminati', the great faceless conglomerate who pull the strings and conceal information that we, the public, are deemed unfit to handle? One thing that does ring true is that the scientific descendants of Crosse did succeed in reproducing at least some of the steps required to replicate the process of life.

Chapter 24
Charles Darwin: The Beginning

For many centuries, belief in the biblical version of our origins was so much easier to accept simply because there was no other choice. There was The Creation, the Garden of Eden, Adam and Eve, Eve's temptation of Adam which incurred God's wrath and led to them being cast out of paradise. All allegories and myths, but although still a major part of the fundamentalist canon of belief, this blissful state of ignorance was, at least in previous centuries, fairly easy to maintain simply because people would not even think to question biblical teaching. To do so, especially in medieval times, would have invited charges of heresy and a certain way of seeing the inside of a torture chamber, and perhaps a hellish death at the stake. Although as the decades and centuries passed and superstition began to fade through education, people could perhaps question traditional teachings, but since they could come up with nothing better they had to accept what they had until the advent of Darwin.

Born in Shropshire to a wealthy family, Darwin attended an elite private school from where he graduated to Edinburgh University to study medicine. This choice of career evidently did not suit him, so, in 1827 he entered Cambridge University with the intention of becoming a clergyman in the Church of England, and while there he met two men who proved pivotal in his career. They were Adam Sedgwick and John Henslow, one a geologist, the other a naturalist. From them Darwin learned the basic skills and techniques required in collecting and mounting specimens. Graduating from Cambridge in 1831 aged only 22, Darwin was taken on board the English survey ship, the HMS Beagle, as an unpaid naturalist.

It was during this voyage that he was, as a result of his findings, forced to confront the perceived wisdom of the era, the so-called *'Catastrophist Theory'*. This, along with the Bible, was the corner stone of conventional creationist belief. It postulated that the Earth had experienced a whole succession of creations, each destroyed by a sudden catastrophe. The last cataclysm had been the previously mentioned Great Flood of Noah, which wiped out all life. All the fossils unearthed by archaeologists constituted the remains of those destroyed in previous disasters. In the view of the Catastrophists and Creationists, all species were created individually and had existed in their original form since the beginning and would remain unchanged forever more. When he returned to England, Darwin set about recording his findings on changeability, finally culminating in his seminal work published in 1879 and entitled *'On the Origin of Species by means of Natural Selection'*. Incidentally, if Noah and his wife and family were the only ones to survive the deluge, surely this must infer that we are all the children of Noah rather then those of Adam?

This work literally struck a hammer blow to accepted wisdom; even his later works including *'The Descent of Man'* did not provoke the same outraged response. The net result of the controversy was the polarization of belief into two camps, i.e. the Creationists and the Evolutionists. At first there was widespread and predictable condemnation from the churches and the scientific establishment. But gradually this theory became grudgingly accepted. However, this was not universal, and in America this led to court cases, most notably the famous 1926 'Scopes Monkey Trial' in Tennessee, which caught the attention and imagination of the world. Proponents of the biblical creationist tradition went to court to prevent the theory of evolution being taught in schools.

The evolutionists case was fought by the famous lawyer, Clarence Darrow. He won and the rest, as they say, is history. Over time, due to logic, education and commonsense, evolution and natural selection obtained respectability. One accepted wisdom was replaced by another but there was a measure of tolerance, at least until another theory arrived, which, in its scope, was even more unsettling than evolution. This was the proposition that we are not children of this planet: our progenitors did not come from this world, our ancestors came from the stars. What follows is another variant explanation of how, apart from the laboratory experiments so far discussed, the human race may have arrived here on the Earth, and in many ways it supplements and enhances the other versions still to come later in these pages.

Chapter 25
Changes

This theory, which is as revolutionary as Darwin's evolution, implies that whoever designed us must have been as genetically similar to us as we are to apes. Depending on how we interpret various biblical statements, especially in the Old Testament, there appears to be frequent mention of interference by extraterrestrials in the origins of modern man. Judeo/Christian belief seems to regard the Old Testament as a bit of an embarrassment and the Christian New Testament contains far fewer references of this kind. This is quite understandable since in the course of many early church councils, most notably *'The Council of Nicea'* in AD 365, where the New Testament was constructed, re-constructed and finally approved.

Bear in mind that the New Testament comprises all the available contemporary information in the shape of written and oral traditions. The written information was in Hebrew, Greek and Latin. There was no punctuation or upper and lower case letters, much was incomplete and the result was a consensus regarding what was or was not true and, it has to be said, expedient; this in turn depended entirely on what was considered suitable and best served the agenda of the newly formed church. Never forget that prior to The Council of Nicea, Christ was a remarkable man but very human; after Nicea he was divine, that is how important and influential this gathering was.

There have been several revisions since; the first on record was not all that long after the prognostications of the Council of Nicea. A section of the gospel of St. Mark evidently did not suit the opinion of Bishop Clement of Alexandria who altered the references to the resurrection of Lazarus in the gospel of Mark. He is on record as saying: *"For even if they should say something true, one who loves the truth should not... agree with them...For not all true things are to be said to all men"*. Evidently the black arts of the spin-doctor were known even then, an attitude that, whilst disturbing, should not come as too much of a surprise. For many centuries the only people with any education to speak of were in the service of the church, and from their perspective this was both acceptable and appropriate since knowledge automatically conferred power. The populace were kept in line and fed whatever version of the 'truth' was deemed suitable; it still happens today and is used by the governments of countries the world over to subjugate and pacify their populations.

Although, as stated at the beginning of this book, I do have reservations about quoting biblical sources, it seems safe to assume that the references to aerial anomalies in the Old Testament are there because the early censors did not, a) understand what they were or b) perceive them as a threat to the status quo. There is a mass of evidence in Genesis, the Dead Sea Scrolls and the book of Enoch, which suggests genetic tampering with the early hominids. Genesis 6:1 tells us, 'The sons of God took wives of the daughters of men which gave birth to the Nephilim'. Who or what were the 'Sons of God'? If they were not angels then what were they? Is this a further clue that we are descended from a race of extraterrestrials, the 'sky people' referred to in the ancient traditions of many cultures, including the Mayans? We are also told in Genesis 6:1, 'And it came to pass when man began to multiply on the face of the Earth, and daughters were born unto them. That the sons of God saw the daughters of men that they were fair and they took them wives of all that they chose.' Genesis 6:4 says'There were Nephilim on the Earth in those days and also after that. When the sons of God came unto the daughters of men and they bare children to them. The same became mighty men, which were of old, men of wisdom.'

This text is totally at odds with traditional Creationist teachings, which makes no mention at all about 'Nephilim' or 'Sons of God' nor any inference that they are one and the same thing; in fact one senses a growing unease and embarrassment within Creationist ranks relating to this section of scripture. As we already saw, the story of Adam and Eve tells us that God took a handful of dust and produced Adam the first man, then from Adam's side God takes a rib and as if by magic we have Eve. This could obviously be interpreted as cloning and/or genetic manipulation and in this context is important because it would fit the scenario we are considering. Also of interest is the unambiguous statement, *'And also after that'*. One must assume from this clear statement that these Nephilim were on the earth for some considerable period of time. Surprising though this is, of more interest to us is when did this happen?

Chapter 26
When Time Began?

As we saw in Chapter 19, certain Christian biblical sources give the date of the creation of the world as 4004 BC; some Creationists have it at 10,000 BC and a few Jewish sources are slightly different, the most recent placing it precisely at 3760 BC. According to all these remarkably specific accounts, we and all of creation appeared after six days of God's labor, presumably in His image and looking much as we do now. Therefore, by inference God looks like us, or if not God then our creator(s). If the biblical version is to be accepted there was nothing before these dates, nothing at all, a vacuum *('all was void')*.

This, strangely enough, is quite in keeping with current theories about the 'Big Bang', which, although orders of magnitude older than the alternative calculations, still maintains the religious connection. It is the brainchild of a Jesuit named Lemaitre and proposes that prior to the seething maelstrom of creation there was absolutely nothing, not even the space that the universe expanded into. We are now as we were then at the point of creation, there was no evolution, no change. Creationism was the accepted teaching until Darwin appeared with his theories of evolution and natural selection and changed all that and pushed back the date of our origins. Over millennia we evolved from apes, through Neanderthal man, (so named after a skeleton found in the Neander Valley in Germany). Continuing the evolutionary process into *Homo Erectus,* then *Homo Sapiens* finally culminating in Cro-Magnon Man.

There are two distinct strains, Neanderthal and Cro-Magnon

man. Neanderthal man (although it has now been demonstrated that this species were not nearly as primitive as was at first believed) died out, but Cro-Magnon flourished. This presents a convenient explanation that neatly squares away the loose ends, but what it does not do is explain is why, relatively quickly, *Homo Erectus* developed a larger brain (50% larger), a modern anatomical structure and the ability to use language. This seems to have been achieved in a far shorter timescale than the normal evolutionary process could achieve, so was there intervention and what manner did this intervention take? At first there seems to be two possibilities: on one hand we have the Fallen Angels and on the other there is direct manipulation by extraterrestrials. But perhaps these accounts are the same event described from different perspectives. As an aside it is interesting to note that Neanderthal man had a brain size at least equal to and in many instances larger than ours, so evidently brain size is no guarantee of survival.

The book of Enoch tells us that 200 angels, also known as *'The Watchers,'* rebelled against heavenly laws that required them to accept man as their equal. After being either forcibly ejected from or voluntarily leaving heaven, in a clear and powerful resonance with the Book of Genesis, they took 'wives' among human women. Their offspring were the 'Nephilim'. According to the respected Hebrew researcher and author Zecharia Sitchin, the term 'Nephilim' in Hebrew means *'those who have fallen'*. This in turn translates in Greek as *'Gigantes'*; which is reminiscent of the biblical quotation *'In those days there were giants'*. Are these more references to the Nephilim? The links seem obvious. We are given specific references in the Dead Sea Scrolls to apparent genetic experiments carried out by The Watchers. We are told which animals are selected for this unnatural tampering. These sections are fragmentary: (1Q23 Frag. 1 + 6) *"Two Hundred Donkeys, two hundred asses, two hundred[.....]rams of the flock, two hundred goats, two hundred......beast of the field, from every animal, from every bird ....] [....]for miscegenation[....]".* The scrolls then describe the results of these experiments with animals and human women: *(4Q531 Frag. 2) "[...]They defiled[...] [...] they begot, giants and monsters, they begot, and behold all the Earth was corrupted[....] [....] With its blood and by the hand of [....]giants which did not suffice for them and[...] [....] And they were seeking to devour many[...] [....]the monsters attacked it.*

These fallen angels, who were they? Conspicuous by its absence is the name, Lucifer, (the light bringer); this odd term for Lord of Hell, the epitome of evil and wickedness has always seemed curiously inappropriate and presents entirely the wrong image. In this account the leader was known as Semjaza, his lieutenants were called Azazel, Penemue, and Kasdeja. These fallen angels, in between enjoying the favors of human women, are credited with teaching us various skills. These were, working with metals, basic chemistry, and the use of cosmetics. Azazel in particular taught women to enjoy sex and encouraged promiscuity. The Hebrew storytellers regarded this as a great blasphemy.

More disconcertingly, the fallen angel Kasdeja taught women how to abort children. Why? The teaching of these skills raises a very awkward question. Why would angels – these ethereal creatures – have any need for skills like these; of what possible use were they? Unless of course they were not angels or any other kind of spiritual creature. Rather, they have all the attributes of a highly advanced race passing on whatever knowledge they felt that a more primitive people could absorb. Since the people who recorded these events did not have the vocabulary to adequately describe what they were witnessing, it is little wonder that a more advanced race, with the apparent ability to 'descend from heaven', were viewed as gods and angels. In the meantime, the offspring of the 'fallen ones' i.e. the Nephilim, had begun to attack, kill, and eat mankind.

The angels (or watchers) who had remained loyal to God were

sent to act against their rebellious former colleagues and their offspring who were described as *'the bastards and the reprobates and the children of fornication'*. The loyal watchers were victorious, and the rebels were forced to watch as their offspring were destroyed. For their part the rebels were themselves thrown into a heavenly prison that was reportedly an abyss of fire. From this it would be fair to assume that the rebels were in fact cast down into Hell since there is no mention of it before this. There is a parallel to this in Greek mythology where there is a race of part celestial, part terrestrial beings called *'The Titans'* who performed superhuman feats. Once again it is quite possible that this is the same set of events described from a yet another viewpoint.

Alternatives

In a number of books, the researcher and author, Zecharia Sitchin, has put forward the theory that there was no super-natural involvement in the origins of the human race. According to him, and strongly supporting what we have already seen, we are the products of genetic manipulation by a race known as *'The Annunaki'*. He states that this word translates as *'Those who from Heaven to Earth fell'*. He goes on to claim that there is a twelfth planet, *'Nibiru,'* which comes within range of Earth every 3600 years. The technology of this race when they first came here was not all that far ahead of our own as it is at present. He bases this on scriptural accounts of vehicles that apparently roared and belched flame. These seem similar to what our technology has produced in terms of reaction-powered space-going vehicles that have taken us to the moon and continue to propel experimental craft around and out of the solar system. Presumably the science of this race would now be far ahead of ours and it would be arrogant of us to presume that our ability to understand it is any better than that of our forefathers.

Sitchin claims that our technology has taken a step change approximately every 3600 years, which coincides with both the arrival of this mysterious planet 'Nibiru' within our solar system and contact with its inhabitants. One fascinating common thread running through all these theories and opinions is that they all point to the possibility that we were visited in the dawn of history by a race that was not from this world. They have different names, as do the results of their genetic meddling, the Fallen Angels, Annunaki, Nephilim, Elohim and Titans, but they all amount to the same thing. The only difference is the point of view and level of technology of the observers. In other words the great common denominator of 'context', something that appears repeatedly throughout this book.

It is worth mentioning that in America the Creationists have not given up. In the state of Kansas the same argument is brewing again about evolutionary theory being taught in schools. Once again Christian fundamentalists are up in arms and prefer to believe in the literal truth of the Bible. They are again outraged at a conventional secular curriculum being taught in schools. Many Christian students are currently openly questioning the standard theory of evolution as something they do not and cannot accept. Their teachers liken the process of educating these children to hitting their heads against a brick wall, but unfortunately the American Constitution guarantees that the Creationists have every right to have their bizarre version of prehistory taught alongside what is scientifically demonstrable. Bear in mind that they also fully accept that Adam and Eve were the first inhabitants of the Earth and, unlikely as it may seem, every one that now inhabits the planet must therefore be their descendants. The subject of how the human race may have arrived on the Earth is discussed in more detail in the next three chapters.

Chapter 27
Panspermia; In Our Image and Likeness?

'Let us make man in our image, after our likeness', so says Genesis 1:26 according to the King James translation of the Bible, another comment on what God looks like, and quite specifically suggesting that either we are in the physical image of our creator, or the idea of a 'Royal We' is infinitely older and much more widespread than we first thought and there was more than one creator. 'Not so', say the Creationists, who insist that any reference to a similarity in appearance is intended as an allegory and indicates a spiritual likeness and not any physical similarity. Note that this seems to be counter to their Adam and Eve hypothesis whose appearance must presumably have been designed on some arbitrary whim. Why should this be? Is it because this is extremely convenient and tidies away any loose ends and allows them to ignore all the science suggesting just the opposite?

Interestingly, the opening quotation goes on to say that the human race, or 'man', should have dominion over all other species on the planet, and this is found in all the other official translations of scripture. Unfortunately, certain fundamentalist nominally Christian racist groups also use this quotation to help justify their unsavory views on those who are not of Caucasian descent. It also seems to indicate that even Creationists are selective in which parts of scripture they deem suitable for use as examples of literal truth, since if we are indeed physically similar to whatever created us then this also raises some difficult questions and only serves to further 'humanize' and somehow disenfranchise their version of God. What it also appears to do is legitimize the ideas of such supposedly heretical medieval schisms as the Cathars, whose dualistic system of worship claimed that there were two version of God, one physical, the *Rex Mundi* or God of the World, and one spiritual who, since there was no trace of corporeality, was the only genuinely pure spirit. According to this philosophy, since Christ was a physical manifestation of God, he could not be perfect. The Catholic Church viewed this as the ultimate heresy, and after repeated warnings to desist, instituted the Albigensian Crusade. This, in turn, lead to the total physical suppression of the Cathars, who, nonetheless, are still remembered through their teachings. This is another example of the many repeated throughout history of removing dissent by the simple expedient of murdering those who spread it.

The notion of panspermia does have one particular advantage in that as well as providing samples of our creators DNA it helps to take chance out of the equation; but equally it introduces another possibly unpalatable factor, that we are, literally, children of the cosmos. But for some sections of the population even this idea does not answer all parts of the puzzle. They still see a slight element of risk in the process, so they take the concept of panspermia and add to it by coming up with the idea of *'directed panspermia'*, or the deliberate and calculated seeding of our planet using, let's call them *'life packets'*. This has obvious attractions, but as with many revolutionary ideas it also introduces a number of other questions, like why this particular planet? Is it because of the so-called 'Goldilocks Zone' or the planetary position of the Earth in relation to the Sun, not too hot, not too cold, just enough oxygen, just enough water etc? Bear in mind that all this would have occurred after the prolonged 'settling in' process.

Much more likely using this scenario is that a large number of 'life packets' were dispatched more or less at random to land where they would and, if the conditions were right, develop. Does this infer that the creation of the solar system and its planets and even the 'Late Heavy Bombardment' was actually a deliberate part of the seeding process? Of course this assumes that the 'life packets' were more or less uniform and contained the same or similar ingredients, which in this case may imply that all life in the universe must be basically the same. The other alternative is that the 'life packets' contained a range of building blocks suitable for a wide range of conditions. In other words, irrespective of where the 'packets' arrived they contained the raw material to create life, where life, *any form of life,* was possible.

This introduces the ultimate question: who sent the 'packets' and why did they send them? But before we look at this there is yet another question. According to our cosmology the universe in which we live came into being at the beginning of time when the 'Big Bang' occurred and the constituent parts of the universe erupted from the miniscule singularity at its core. From what is known – or perhaps hypothesized might be a better description – of this event it is assumed that the matter forming the universe and all it contains was created in literally nanoseconds from the super-dense core singularity. Does this mean that all the gases, elements and particles arrived in their places uniformly at the same instant?

We know this is not the case, because many millions of planets and stars are of various ages and the Earth is relatively young in planetary terms (e.g. our sun is still in its healthy early middle age); so we can also safely assume that there are planets and suns out there that are very much older. This also applies to suns in other galaxies, many of which have long used up their fuel and burned out and are in the process of collapsing to create 'black holes'. In fact we can sometimes witness the destruction of stars in the form of novas and supernovas, safe in the knowledge that they are trillions and billions of miles away, separated from our solar system in distances measured in light years. The black holes were recognized and named when physicists and astronomers realized that the irregular movements of some planets had to be caused by the presence of massive but invisible gravity fields that both capture and bend light in their vicinity.

All this goes to suggest that we as a race are comparatively recent arrivals and since there are many much older suns and plants it is reasonable to suggest that there are likewise much older civilizations and it may be that it is these civilizations that sent out the 'life packets' by their tens of thousands to wander the stygian void of the universe seeking a fertile nursery. Does this mean that this seminal 'mother race' predates all other life in the universe and developed at a much faster rate than all the other races and civilizations that surely exist? If the answer is no then this leads to even more wondrous possibilities, but for the present let's assume that the answer is yes. The mother race is by definition extraterrestrial and not only is it extraterrestrial, presumably it is 'extra' to all other civilizations elsewhere in the universe; it would have to be if it seeded them as well. Might it possible that what has been discussed here so far only applies to this universe, but not to the other universes that are theorized to exist concurrently with our own? Might the inhabitants of the alternate universes want to move here, into our reality, and have prepared the environment? Even more astounding, are they already here and have been since the very beginning, in other words, did they become us? This is one of the puzzles we will examine as we continue through these pages.

In addition, there are a few truly breathtaking aspects of the relationship between physical reality and the cold, hard, facts as embodied in mathematical principles. An example of this is the strange and haunting musical properties of the DNA molecule, this graceful double spiral can be rendered into music using suitable computer software. The same is true of endlessly repeating phenomenon of fractal patterns and the 'Golden Mean', which is a mathematical constant found throughout the cosmos: why? Is it the very idea that all we survey from the microscopic to the cosmic has, as we understand it, to obey the same basic physical laws in order to exist in this universe? The only place where these laws do not always apply is in the arcane alternate reality of quantum physics and it is from this state of flux that our physical reality emerges. This is an apparent dichotomy, but it is also an absolute fact.

The same mathematical patterns are known to exist in language, something that was noted by our ancestors when they created the art of numerology, which relates the spoken word to repeating patterns of numerical values rendering phrases with the same or similar meanings to the same mathematical values. Although there are some linguistic variants on this, basically the letters are assigned a number and when the number of letters in each word, sentence or phrase is counted, they have the same totals. This is of course a simplified explanation, but the meaning is clear. Our universe and all it contains appears to be a rational, calculated, deliberate and premeditated act of creation by a 'Mother Race'.

Perhaps one of the best arguments that the human race was not a creation of sheer chance comes from the work of the French biophysicist de Nouy, who calculated that if all the varied combinations of chemicals in protein chains required to create life were assembled every millionth of a second it would take longer than the planet has been in existence. This of course refers to an utterly and totally unique combination of chemicals that can reproduce copies of itself. Chance or something else? Finally and much more recently, Prof. John Parnell conducted an experiment using sections of rock etc attached to atmospheric re-entry vehicles, which seems to prove that the microbes and chemicals required to create life *could* survive the temperatures created on entry into the Earth's atmosphere. This certainly lends much more weight to panspermia, directed or otherwise.

Chapter 28
Spaceship in the Night Sky

As regards the notion of panspermia as the means of producing human life here on Earth, in the present context it becomes increasingly feasible; but there is one other possibility we might still consider and it is this. If directed panspermia is the correct option and we take the random element out of the equation, might the means of its delivery still be relatively very close at hand, 240,000 miles away in fact, above us in the sky – the Moon. What if the Moon was deliberately steered through the cosmos and 'parked' in orbit around the Earth bringing with it the seeds of life, or alternatively, was the moon used as living quarters for those who tended and readied the planet for seeding?

Might they have been the scientists who observed the reactions of the chemical compounds in the organic fog that covered the surface? This hypothesis might explain why, rather than just dump us here in our current form, it suited their ends much better to bring about our creation through the slow process of gradual evolution. This suggests that if it was better to allow us to develop all the way from 'dead chemicals' into something that is alive, then assuming then the Earth was, in effect, a laboratory, then the previously discussed Miller-Urey experiment was on the right lines. It also helps to lend credence to the hypothesis that when life was seeded into the universe it was done in a manner that was most likely to take root in the most hospitable conditions.

Following detailed examination of the rock and dust samples brought back from various moon missions, it has been determined that the moon is much older than at first thought. The Earth is reckoned to be at least 4.8 to 5 billion years old; moon rocks were dated at 5.3 billion years old and the moondust on which they lay at least 1 billion years older still. Until now it was generally assumed that, as we have already considered, the moon was created by excess material thrown off, (a) during a collision or, (b) by the remains of what struck us. What has to be accepted though is that absolutely nothing could have survived the supposed impact. However, presented with this fresh geological information gleaned from the moon rocks, we now find some extremely interesting questions regarding both the true origins of the moon and the age of planet Earth. It also queries how the moon became trapped in the Earth's gravitational pull.

1) The composition of the rocks and the surrounding dust is markedly different, which indicates that the accepted theory stating that the dust was formed from degradation of the rocks themselves is wrong and the rocks originated elsewhere.

2) Some of the moon rocks were magnetic, which is odd since the moon itself has no discernible magnetic field.

3) The presence of Moon 'Mascons', a name given to large, circular, dense masses of unknown composition lying forty to fifty miles below the centers of the moon's maria (seas). They could be interpreted as artificial since it cannot be coincidental or accidental that each mare has a mascon centered like a bull's-eye beneath it.

4) It is a matter of record that the seismic monitors left on the moon by successive teams of astronauts have recorded meteoric impacts upon the lunar surface that caused the

moon to *'Ring like a bell.'* This was particularly true when on completion of its mission, an unmanned lunar surveyor was allowed to crash on to the lunar surface to provide an impact of known weight.

5) The moon's surface is also much harder than expected; when the astronauts experienced extreme difficulty drilling into the surface of a mare, it was discovered that the surface was composed of 'illeminite', a mineral containing large quantities of titanium. The metal, titanium, is used by the aerospace industry the world over in the construction of high-flying, high performance aircraft like the Lockheed SR 71 Blackbird spy plane and many other military aircraft since.

6) Also found in the lunar rocks were quantities of Uranium 236 and Neptunium 237, neither substance is found naturally on Earth.

7) In addition to these substances there are other metals and minerals that do not occur in nature on the Earth, so where did they come from?

These are a few of many odd and anomalous findings made by NASA – or at least they are the findings they have seen fit to release into the public domain. If, as suggested, the moon is artificial in the sense that it may have been hollowed out and brought here into Earth's orbit, if it was brought here, then someone, or something, had to steer it. Is there any evidence of them? In addition, if the age of the recovered moon artefacts is accurate, then this also surely corroborates the evidence that the discrepancies in the age of the universe are real and our moon may have originated in a different part of the cosmos. There is abundant anecdotal evidence originating from former NASA employees and also the astronauts themselves, that there are signs of habitation on the moon. If one considers the arguments that the Moon is hollow, then it becomes possible that it did serve as a gigantic spacecraft for some ancient and advanced race that brought it to our solar system to either establish themselves here on Earth or nurture the fledgling life as it developed. What evidence is there that the moon has been inhabited by an unknown race and used as transport for them?

It is by convention that we believe man visited the moon for the first time in 1969. Of the three astronauts on the Apollo 11 mission, Neil Armstrong, Edwin Eugene 'Buzz' Aldrin and Michael Collins, the command module pilot, Collins, remained in orbit while his two companions, Neil Armstrong and 'Buzz' Aldrin, both former US Air force fighter pilots, actually landed in a tiny 'LEM' or Lunar Excursion Module and walked on the airless, dusty surface of the moon. For what it's worth, I am old enough to remember staying up to watch the TV images sent from the lunar landing site and being suitably impressed. To think of questioning whether or not this was genuine never occurred to me – but perhaps we lived in slightly less paranoid and more trusting times. This of course is not to say that the governments and security services of all countries do not lie to their citizens, because they do, regularly and often; it used to be called propaganda, but is now known as 'information management'.

We are told that the last manned mission to land on the moon was in 1972 and since then, due mainly to spiraling costs, we have never repeated this feat despite current technology being infinitely better. For example, it has been stated that modern, hand held games consoles like the 'Nintendo Game Boy' and even digital watches possess considerably more computing power than the first manned space missions. Although the memory of these historic missions has faded into the background now, there are aspects that still gnaw at us. Despite repeated and probably necessary denials from NASA, an increasing body of evidence has grown suggesting that, as we will discover, there was evidence of habitation already present on the moon and the astronauts witnessed it.

We cannot have it both ways here, because the claims of one camp are totally at odds with those of the other; either we did go to the moon and the astronauts did see these artefacts, or we did not and the claims made by various researchers (and supposedly the astronauts) are totally bogus. The arguments of the 'landing skeptics' about the ability of human organisms to survive the radiation in deep space hold that we as a species cannot do this and are not designed to do so. On the other hand we can and do send our scientists and technicians to the International Space Station for weeks and months at a time with no lasting ill effects. This seems to be argument enough that given the appropriate protection we can indeed survive the rigors of life in space. This being the case, I am willing to accept the premise that we did visit the moon and anomalies were discovered, but that information was deliberately withheld.

All through the Apollo missions there have been suspicions of an ongoing cover up of varying degrees whether relating to alleged UFO sightings made by the astronauts whilst in transit, or to reports of structures on the moon. A former official of the ground-based NASA monitoring team, Otto Bender, reported that certain transmissions made by Armstrong and Aldrin were allegedly subject to NASA censorship and as result never heard by the general public. The following information is sourced from individuals who were in possession of their own VHF receiving equipment and therefore able to monitor NASA communications feeds. This type of monitoring, due to vastly more secure digital and encrypted communication systems, would be considerably more difficult, if not impossible, to repeat nowadays.

According to these sources, monitoring staff quickly cut off the conversations between the astronauts and NASA. Bender stated, "This conversation presumably took place when the two moon walkers, Armstrong and Aldrin were on the surface, some distance from the LEM Armstrong clutched Aldrin's arm and exclaimed, "What was it? What the hell was it? That's all I want to know". This was followed by another exchange,

MISSION CONTROL: *"What's there...(garble)...Mission Control calling Apollo 11..."*
APOLLO 11: *"These babies are huge sir...enormous... oh God, you wouldn't believe it...I'm telling you there are other spacecraft out there...lined up on the far side of the crater edge...they're on the moon watching us..."*

A statement attributed to a leading space research scientist, Dr. Garry Henderson says:

"All our astronauts have seen these objects, but have been ordered not to discuss their findings with anyone".

Unsurprisingly, NASA has never confirmed this account, but perhaps significantly shortly after their return, Buzz Aldrin complained that; *"The agency is using us as goddam traveling salesmen"*. Aldrin, following bouts of heavy drinking, was eventually hospitalized suffering from 'emotional depression'. One interpretation of his comments insinuates that the expression 'traveling salesman' was a reference to NASA selling their version of the truth and denying the existence of an extraterrestrial presence. Another and probably more rational explanation holds that NASA, in order to justify their ever increasing budget, was presenting the astronauts to the worlds press and media at every and any opportunity.

Was the moonwalk merely an elaborate and hugely expensive exercise in public relations aimed at justifying their [NASA's] allocation of government funds? The experience of traveling to

Earth's nearest neighbor the moon appears to have had a powerful effect on several astronauts, for example James Irwin, the sixth man to walk on the moon's surface. Irwin, in May 1972, resigned from the NASA space program to become a Baptist missionary commenting, *"The flight made me a more deeply religious person and more keenly aware of the fragile nature of the planet"*. This deep emotional effect is not really surprising given that anyone experiencing the magnitude of space and the stark reality of man's place in the universe is bound to experience some degree of cathartic reaction. Indeed the failure to do so must indicate complete emotional anesthesia in the observer.

Another drop-out was Apollo 14 astronaut Edgar (Ed) Mitchell who also resigned in 1979 to study parapsychology, founding the 'New Age' research centre known as *'The Institute of Noetic Sciences'* near San Francisco in America. Mitchell describes his impressions of the Earth when viewed from the Moon, *"I went into a very deep pathos, a kind of anguish. The incredibly beautiful planet that is Earth, a place no bigger than my thumb was my home... a blue and white jewel against a black velvet sky...was being killed off"*. Interestingly, a British newspaper, the Daily Express, also attributed the following statement to him; *" In order to survive, society has three ways to go, and the third is the most viable but most difficult alternative"*. This comment is assumed to refer to a series of clandestine proposals culminating in what is now referred to as *'Alternative Three.'* This odd expression, 'Alternative Three', refers to an alleged and highly dubious idea designed to overcome overpopulation on the Earth by colonizing the planet Mars. Bob Grodin, another Apollo moon walker, when interviewed by Sceptre Television prior to airing a TV program entitled 'Alternative Three' on June 20 1977 said, *"Do you think they need all that crap down in Florida just to put two guys up there on a...on a bicycle? The hell they do. You know why they need us? So they got a good PR story for all that hardware they've been firing into space, we're nothing man, nothing!"*

Later in 1977 on the 11th of July, the Los Angeles Times published an interview with Dr. Gerard O'Neill a Princeton University Professor. Dr. O'Neill who also served as a professor of Aerospace at MIT, (the Massachusetts Institute of Technology), was also receiving research grants of almost $500,000 per year from NASA, (that amounts to more than $6,000,000 or £2,600,000 in today's terms). In the interview, Dr. O'Neill's comments on world population in 1979 seemed ridiculous at that time. He stated, *"The world's population, currently about 4 billion will, by the year 2000, stand at around 6.5 billion"*, a prophecy that has proved remarkably accurate. He pointed out that, at that time in percentage terms, thirty percent of the population was in developed nations and went on, *"Because of the projected population growth in undeveloped countries this will drop to around 22% by the end of the 20th century. The world will be a hungrier and poorer place"*.

He also commented on the now well-documented effects of pollution and greenhouse gases which resulted in the notorious and much hyped 'greenhouse effect'. From our position of over thirty years in the future we can reflect on just how accurate these comments and observations were; Dr. O'Neill's solution to the problem? *'Island 3.'* He said, *"There's no doubt about the technology, it's already in place, that's been confirmed by NASA, it's all ready to go"*. There can be little doubt that O'Neill's enthusiastic remarks give credence to the previously mentioned Alternative Three. Alternative Three was a proposal that caused all sorts of frantic speculation and has since been shown to be a hoax, was the idea that the human race could travel to the planet Mars, which would be 'terraformed' in the biggest and most complex civil engineering project ever attempted. Apart from the mind numbing logistics involved in such a venture, there have been suggestions quite unrelated to the supposed project involving seeding the Martian atmosphere with algae and other organic agents. In an operation, which resonates with the 'red weed' in HG Well's *'The War of The Worlds'*, the idea was to allow the exported organic matter and organisms, to, over time, slowly alter the atmosphere and surface of the planet into an environment more suited to human habitation.

This was a speculative response to the prophesied overpopulation of our planet and the continuing and increasing depletion of precious resources. Although a hoax, as time passes – and there is, as yet, no general agreement on either overpopulation or dwindling resources – perhaps engineers and scientists may yet be forced to consider whether a proposal such as 'Alternative Three' is indeed viable. This is not as nonsensical as it first appears either; it has frequently been suggested that the writers of science fiction and fantasy may be 'drip fed' information from sources unknown to bring it to the attention of the public in the form of fiction. This is rather in the manner of the speculative writing of Jules Verne and H. G Wells and the other founding fathers of the Sci-Fi genre, some of whose imaginings are now commonplace.

If, as we have seen, there are reasons to believe that the moon may not have be the inadvertent offspring of the Earth's creation and that there are still traces of visits by another race, just how seriously should we take them. Are these 'extraterrestrial races' acting in our best interests, or is the moon merely a convenient hideaway, a 'cosmic motel' for them and their craft while they carry out enigmatic projects here on the Earth. Or, even more strangely, are they the descendants of the race (or races) who actually placed the moon in Earth's orbit in the first place and who still monitor the project aeons after it was begun?

Chapter 29
The Mother Race

What then of this 'Mother Race', how should we consider them? For even assuming that they were responsible for sending various kinds of life out into the universe where did they come from? Were they the chance product of a chemical soup, or are they also the product of outside help? The subject is like the layers of an onion – peel away one and there is another inside; but even an onion has a finite number of layers and can be quickly stripped back to nothing. Did this mother race exist quite independently of the rest of creation? Or did they exist in some parallel reality and entered our universe shortly after its creation? If they did exist alongside us then it may have been in their interest to ensure the propagation of life, not only in this universe but in all the others too. This would account for the diversity of life allegedly existing in other realms that conforms to an approximately humanoid template; but what of the existence of other, non-human and indeed non-carbon based life. Is it likely that we would recognize it as life even if we saw it? Is it so utterly alien to our preconceptions of life that we fail to see it even when it is right in front of us?

Questions like this cause us to speculate on whether alleged visits from ET's to this planet are analogous with parental care when a parent keeps a check on how its child is behaving? Are we still regarded as juveniles and not to be trusted to run our own affairs? It has to be said that our traits are not those of maturity, but rather the opposite as we squabble and quarrel among ourselves over power, land and resources. Perhaps we need parental guidance to stop us from doing this. The assumed role of ET has in general been one of a moral and ethical guide, much in the same manner as visions of the Blessed Virgin Mary (BVM) have appeared from time to time alternately admonishing and threatening us over our stupidity and venality. ET's or mystical beings: that is at the very nub of the matter. Both fill the role of something from 'out there' sent to help us see reason; both have played their role in our creation; and both are worshipped as divine. The only difference here is in the context.

Perhaps it is worth considering that what has previously been assumed to be visits from 'divine beings' was nothing of the kind, because in nearly all cases these entities share virtually identical characteristics with both ET's and ED's (extradimensionals). It is probably no coincidence that a series of alleged visitations by the BVM at Fatima in Portugal, especially the final one, have more in common with UFO contact that any spiritual encounter. It once again demonstrates that there is often absolutely no difference between ET's and angels except in context and the cultural leanings of those who have the encounter. We cannot assume and for good reason too, that we are not the 'original design' to appear on the Earth. We know from our own lengthy and painstaking research that we were preceded by a series of 'prototypes', successful and otherwise. Everything from the early hominids that developed from even more primitive species to *Homo erectus* through Neanderthal man to Cro-Magnon man and eventually to what we are now. As we now know, for various reasons the others died out leaving modern man and our cousins, the great apes, that evolved along a separate and parallel path.

What we have seen here is the difficulty inherent in discussing matters such as this, extricating them from religion and superstition and trying to examine the diverse phenomena in a rational and open-minded manner, and even science cannot explain some of the puzzles. The case is not helped by the fact that there is no traditional bond between religion and science, which should be no surprise given that traditionally they have ways made uneasy bedfellows. The annals of history are full of instances where scientists were tortured and murdered in the name of religion when they rejected accepted dogma because they could prove it to be wrong. However, science and scientists are, in their own way, locked in their own versions of convention and dogma and, in the main, reject the possibility of the arrival of life from outside the confines of the planet. This does of course raise the possibility that if life did arise spontaneously from the elements comprising the planet, since the planet formed from cosmic debris, then it did, in that sense, arrive from the cosmos.

We can also deduce that if life did arise in the manner that the evolutionists suggest, then it was an absolutely unique event, because it has not happened since the original event anywhere else on Earth, in or out of a laboratory, the Miller-Urey experiment notwithstanding. This is of course not to say that the conditions cannot be reproduced artificially. Are we now as our designers intended us to be? The futurists of the late 19th and early 20th centuries used to envisage an age where the human race had evolved to the point where our heads were huge and our bodies were relatively weak and spindly, almost analogous to the ubiquitous 'grays' associated with UFO sightings etc. One avowed Evolutionist, Professor Steve Jones, who runs the Department of Genetics, Evolution and the Environment at University College in London thinks that, at least in the West, we have almost reached the end of the line as far as our evolution is concerned. His hypothesis, which is extremely plausible, suggests that as our medical skills have developed we have effectively altered and subverted the three factors that are vital to evolution, i.e. natural selection, mutation and random change, allowing them to decrease and as such perhaps unhealthy and unfit strains are allowed to remain. To think or consider otherwise nowadays has become anathema since the 'caring and inclusive society' in which we live insists that all, even the patently unsuited must be included, cared for and accepted into the gene pool. While this is laudable and correct using current values, what of the future? What happens when nature is not allowed to make the choices, what happens when the gene pool becomes so debased through misplaced kindness that fitness and suitability are determined solely by the use of prostheses and other aids to permit such basic functions as walking and lifting?

What happens when the population far outstretches the capacity of the planet to provide sustenance for it? According to Professor Jones, if human beings had remained as isolated groups of hunter-gatherers and had not developed agriculture, farming and animal husbandry, the population of the entire planet would be around a half million people, or the population of a small city. The downside of this is that since life would of necessity have been lived more or less from hand to mouth, the groups would have been largely nomadic and tended to gravitate to where life was easiest for them in the forests and near the coast. Those who comprised these groups would have been more liable to mutation and natural selection and may have looked quite different from us. Any technology that might have developed would have been based on different imperatives predicated on what was required for survival.

If Professor Jones is correct, it may take another global cataclysm to restart the evolutionary process and finally permit us to become as our creators intended us to be, whatever form that may take. There is however one nagging doubt: in 1900 Lord Kelvin, one of the great and good in science and physics, commented in a remarkable display of arrogance that, *'There is nothing new to be discovered in physics'*, implying that everything that could be invented had been invented and within his understanding of the physical sciences he may even have been partly justified in his prognosis. An example of this were the assurances that heavier than air machines could not fly, how could they, it defied all logic? He and his colleagues should really have known better, for they had already achieved the impossible in terms of the dreams of their scientific predecessors. It was not until shortly after this that a series of breakthroughs were made in different disciplines within their own professions, especially particle physics, that new and undreamed of areas of exploration were revealed and those who made the initial discoveries were perhaps considered as heretics by those who did not want to see beyond their own comfortable borders.

~

Section Four

Past Remembered Days

~

Chapter 30
Into the Fourth Dimension

In this, the fourth and last section of this book, we embark upon yet more facets of the rapidly filling theatre of the damned; in this case we enter the supposedly respectable world of science to encounter aspects of this discipline that border, if not actually encroach, upon the world of magic and magicians. The reason will become obvious, for it is through the endeavors of those engaged in research into the exotic and indeed esoteric aspects of the nature of reality who will eventually strip away the blinkers we wear to reveal the truth that the ancients instinctively knew was there. It is the physicists and scientists in their laboratories who are fast becoming the new magicians and shamans and it is they who will one day, perhaps soon, reveal that we can alter matter in response to an act of will. Perhaps Aleister Crowley's idea of 'Thelema' was not so wide of the mark after all. The difference here is that it will no longer be a matter of luck and strange rituals, it will be the simple act of flicking a switch to activate a machine. When that arrives men will truly be gods, we will be our own creators and, who knows, perhaps this has already happened somewhere in our future; and history will, as it has in the past, be repeating itself, and if this is the case, is humanity the architect of its own damnation?

One of the most unlikely of all the convoluted aspects of 'superscience' i.e. the kind of technology that allegedly permits alien spacecraft to visit the planet Earth, is the enigma of 'time travel', or the ability to move from the present day to a set point either in the past or the future. It is a subject that has fascinated science fiction writers since the genre was created and was celebrated by the author, HG Wells, in his classic novel, *'The Time Machine'*, which went on to be filmed twice. The manner in which Wells imagined his apparatus was very much a product of the 19th century in Victorian Britain, a mechanical device that seems to have used the then fledgling and mysterious science of electricity as it source of power. This was admirably recreated by the special effects designers in the first George Pal version of the film made in 1960, where it resembles a kind of partially enclosed sleigh with a large rotating disc at the rear. The 2002 remake directed by Simon Wells, the grandson of the author, features a similar construction, but in this case light and rotating prisms appear to provide the motive force. In both examples, the inventor climbs aboard, sets the desired date on a dial, then commences his journey by pulling on a short lever. The concept of a time traveling vehicle or machine has been used many times since in number of guises in various science fiction films.

For Wells to have even contemplated such a scheme speaks volumes for his imagination and perhaps prescience, when the concept was considered utterly impossible by the science of his era. But now, using the arcane calculations of quantum mechanics, the idea becomes at least theoretically possible. Unfortunately, although to actually construct a device capable of bringing this about is, for all practical purposes, highly unlikely, it has not stopped people from claiming that they have indeed done so using two quite clearly defined processes. One method apparently assumes that it is entirely possible to move a physical body in both space and time, while the other claims to move only consciousness and awareness, which on the face of it seems to be the more attractive and attainable proposition.

The Travelers

One of those who claim to have physically traveled in time is one John Titor, an enigmatic character supposedly from 2036, whose assertions appeared briefly between January and March 2001 in a series of posts on an Internet time travel site. These featured a considerable amount of semi-scientific jargon and borrowed heavily from the theorizing and musings of modern physicists. An example of this is a direct reference to the ideas of, amongst others, the physicist Frank Tipler, who postulated that a mile long cylinder composed of extremely dense material, like the stuff of dwarf stars, spinning at near light speed would create the conditions (i.e. a powerful, localized, gravity field) causing a breach in space-time.

Titor's acknowledgement of Tipler came in the shape of an unexplained concept called a *'Tipler Sinusoid'*, and a nod to other physicists came from the application of *'rotating micro-miniature singularities'*. These, he insisted, were present in the device he used, which, incongruously, resembled a small rectangular box. Like Tipler's spinning cylinder these would have the necessary ability to generate the gravity forces required to rupture space/time. But since they are in effect 'black holes', just how they were supposed to be used, let alone controlled, is something of a mystery. Whether Titor's claims were nothing more than a hoax is beside the point since the entire subject is riven with speculation and conjecture anyway; nevertheless at the time the concept attracted considerable interest and indeed still does.

Views of The Apocalypse

As it happens, at the time of writing there was a great furor concerning the impending activation of the European Large Hadron Collider (LHC), which is situated on the Swiss/French border. This gigantic and hugely expensive underground toroidal machine, (it is seventeen miles long), which was built by the European Organization for Nuclear Research (CERN), is intended to advance our understanding of the fundamental particles in the universe by colliding protons at near light speed and creating the conditions present immediately after the 'big bang', this it is hoped will prove the existence of, amongst other particles, the so-called 'Higgs Boson'. This theoretical particle, which is named after Dr. Peter Higgs the physicist who theorized its existence, is assumed to give other particles their mass and therefore weight.

The fear is that, once activated, the LHC might also create an unstable miniature black hole and lead to the ultimate destruction of the Earth. Those who accept this possibility worry that due to the incredible density and weight of the black hole irrespective of size, it could not be contained by the superconducting magnetic fields surrounding the LHC and would literally fall through the walls of the Collider and into the Earth. This would lead to the planet being sucked piecemeal into its ravenous maw from the inside out. It was a similar mindset considered by the physicist, Edward Teller, who predicted that the first ever nuclear explosion during the Manhattan Project might ignite the atmosphere and extinguish all life on the planet: it did not. With this in mind and assuming the worst does not happen, the LHC might just provide unexpected insights into time travel. Incidentally, fear of the unknown was the reason that the maps drawn by early cartographers carried the dire warning that, *'Here be dragons'*, on areas of the ocean that had not been explored.

Oddly enough, in common with the plot device used in another time travel based film, *Back to The Future,* Titor's device was securely attached to a car – in his case a Chevrolet Corvette rather than the ill-fated stainless steel bodied DeLorean used in *Back to The Future,* in which he made his 'time jumps'. He also posted impressive looking diagrams of the object itself on the Internet. Titor's assertions notwithstanding, there is another character claiming to have devised a machine that allows him to liberate his consciousness on the oceans of time. His name is Aage Nost an inhabitant of New Orleans in the USA. The machine Nost constructed does not use pseudo-scientific applications of physics but, instead, appears to be a transmitter of sorts that generates a strong electromagnetic field in the radio frequency (RF) bands. This, he says, allows him to travel at will forward and backwards in time and to observe what is there, and he has publicly demonstrated it many times, including at least once on a television show. Unfortunately the proof relies entirely on the subjective evidence supplied by Nost.

Out of Body Experience

A third claimant to time traveling, who lives in the city of London, is Mr Tony Bassett who calls his device a *'bio-energiser'*. The claims made for the machine have at least been independently tested and appear to be at least partially effective, although Mr Bassett promotes the use of 'guided meditation' as part of the transition process. The introduction of a technique like guided meditation is commonplace with psychologists, counselors and others within the medical support field to induce relaxed mental and physical states conducive to suggestion. Of those who have tried the sessions with Mr Bassett only a very few have actually gone much beyond the instructions given in the guided meditation; but of those who did actually succeed in 'letting go', one described traveling out into deep space among the stars. This should come as no surprise since, as with hypnosis, not everyone is susceptible to suggestion. But this must raise doubts concerning the efficacy of Bassett's machine. Incidentally, the subjects who used the device expressed feelings of incredible loneliness mixed with awe as they gazed on the sheer mind numbing scale of what they saw.

Following a meeting with Hugh Lodge, the nephew of the late Sir Oliver Lodge who, along with the physicist Sir William Crookes was one of the early investigators into psychic phenomena, Mr Bassett developed an interest in the promotion of 'Out Of Body Experiences' (OOBE's). Hugh Lodge introduced him to a process known as the *'Christos Experiment'*, which is a method of inducing OOBE's. These experiences allegedly occur when consciousness leaves the physical body and travels through space and time, which in this context is called 'The Astral Plane'. Bassett used the Christos technique on various people and claims to have had a variable success rate of between 20 to 30%. It may be arguable that the process itself is analogous to the Remote Viewing program instigated by the CIA under the auspices of the previously mentioned *'Stargate Project'*, where operatives were trained to allow their awareness/consciousness to travel to locations indicted by no more than map co-ordinates. Intriguingly, it soon became clear that in a parallel with the claims of Bassett and Nost, the remote viewers could see, not only what was present at the map co-ordinates, but images that were not on this planet, and not even in this time. However the Stargate program was officially closed down and abandoned due to the unreliability of the results, although, to be fair, there were also a few spectacular successes, but not enough to satisfy those funding it.

From the available information, the machine designed by Tony Bassett appears to be a variant on what Aage Nost produced and relies on the generation of a wide range of high frequency EM fields. The claims made for the Bassett and Nost devices may actually have some basis in reality since they can and will induce effects in the brains of those exposed to the radiation rather in the manner of the equipment devised by Prof Michael Persinger, a neuroscientist at the Laurentian University situated in Ontario, Canada. In Prof. Persinger's case the equipment was used to successfully demonstrate that external magnetic fields can produce altered states of perception in people exposed to them. Whether the subjective impressions experienced by the volunteers were purely neurological effects induced by the EM fields themselves, or whether the EM fields somehow retuned the brain to receive another range of inputs is another matter. The only thing one can say with any certainty is that when the EM fields were switched off, the impressions likewise stopped.

Before leaving Tony Bassett and his bio-energiser, at one point he evidently had plans to actually build his device into the walls of a room to act as a permanent installation, although there is no evidence that this was ever done. It is also as well to note that Mr Bassett is acknowledged as a constructor of unique electronic musical instruments, chiefly an oddity called the *'Theremin'.* This 'instrument' has popped up several times over the years and could be regarded, along with the *'Ring Modulator'* and similar devices, as a forerunner of the modern electronic synthesizer. The Theremin was first invented in 1919 by a Russian, Leon Theremin, and is basically two antennae radiating an EM field that respond to the proximity of objects, in this case the human hand.

The musician approached the instrument and 'played' it by altering the proximity of his hands in relation to the antennae thereby altering the EM field; the result was amplified and played over speakers. The sound was, for want of a better word, 'spacey' and rather eerie and featured on the sound tracks of several early Sci-Fi films (including the iconic *The Day the Earth Stood Still*) and radio plays. Its use was also featured in examples of *'musique concrete'* and other forms of electronic music consisting of strange and frequently discordant melodies, pops, screeches, hisses and whistles produced by *avante garde* composers including such UFO luminaries as the late Desmond Leslie. I hasten to add that this observation is by no means designed to diminish the other achievements of Tony Bassett, but only serves to illustrate just how unintentionally synchronous such events can be.

Chapter 31
The Wingmakers

There is yet another case of time travel that might just be relevant here, and that is the odd set of circumstances surrounding what came to be known as *'The Wingmaker Conspiracy'*. This particular set of events, which effectively developed into full-blown New Age cosmology, caused much head scratching and puzzlement on the Internet when it first appeared in the late 1980's, and due to its heretical/technological ethos is worth recounting here because it outlasted the brief supernova that was John Titor. In 1972, a group of vacationers in the wilds of New Mexico accidentally discovered a unique cache of artefacts comprising remarkably well-preserved glyphs drawn on the canyon walls plus a number of objects. Acting responsibly, rather than plunder the site for their own gain, they contacted the University of New Mexico. Intrigued, the university sent an archaeologist to examine the finds, but he could find no obvious signs that any native culture had established an encampment there.

His immediate conclusion was that the objects and the rock drawings were probably created by nomads who had left traces of their presence as they passed through. At first sight this seemed reasonable, but there were inconsistencies. While nearly all of the objects could be dated to around the 8th century AD there was one glaring and anachronistic anomaly, which they named the 'compass artifact'. This particular object was not contemporary with the other items that had been found, i.e. simple tools and pottery shards etc., and appeared to imply a different and possibly higher degree of technology. The 'compass' was covered in inscriptions, and while a few of them matched those on the pottery shards, other illustrations were incompatible with others known to exist in that era; and, stranger still, they did not seem to quite match any others produced by known early cultures in North America.

Someone, probably from the university, must have suspected that something was 'not quite right' here, and since universities and other seats of higher education are frequently linked to the intelligence services, alerted certain agencies within the US Government. Never ones to pass up on anything that might give any kind of military advantage, they became interested – an obsession that is clearly illustrated in other unlikely and borderline magical/occult endeavors it became embroiled in, viz. the Stargate Project *et al.* As a result of its interest, both the artefacts and the find itself were placed under the jurisdiction of the NSA, *(National Security Agency).*

The NSA's involvement was almost certainly due to the glaring discrepancies in the chronology of the finds and a faint possibility that the artefacts and the images were indications of humanity's very early contact with a non-terrestrial race. If this version of events is true it is deeply offensive and truly annoying that we as a race are not deemed ready by our alleged betters to receive information concerning our origins. Whether we evolved from primordial ooze, a Creator God, a passing comet, or through the intervention of a spacefaring race is beside the point, and the only really interested parties are those with something to lose. They are of course the established religions whose function would be rendered superfluous, and of course the legions of believers who, without a godhead would experience a degree of anxiety. In addition, the reputations of many debunking scientists would take a severe bruising.

However, to compensate for this, the religions would probably invent a new belief system much as they largely invented the present one, and the scientists would probably insist they their earlier denials and refutations were misquotes. All that matters is that we as a species survive and hopefully improve. As mentioned elsewhere in this work, we should bear in mind that the US constitution and political system are heavily predicated on religion and its dogma, so it may be that the desire to conceal such contentious matters is fundamental to its existence. Be that as it may, in an attempt to confirm its own suspicions, in 1973 the NSA had the location evaluated again using its own specially commissioned archaeological team, and although a few more pictographs and symbols were located, there was nothing special about them, certainly not enough to either confirm or refute its original suspicions, so no general consensus was reached. As a result of these disappointing results, interest waned and the project was eventually shelved under the code name, *'Ancient Arrow'*. The area of the find was, for no obvious reason, intriguingly declared 'off limits' and forgotten about. Anyone familiar with the paranoia of the intelligence services would not find these actions surprising.

However, in 1994 a landslip revealed a previously unsuspected section of the Ancient Arrow site causing the NSA to reopen the file and dispatch yet another team to the area. This time they discovered the entrance to a tunnel system leading deep into the canyon face. The tunnel was in fact the entrance into many cavities and chambers (twenty three in number) cut deep into the rock. The tunnels were part of a prehistoric mazelike excavation comprising several chambers each containing either a single painting or a series of glyphs plus diagrams/plans resembling examples of an unknown technology. The team immediately contacted their project director, who in turn contacted another alleged NSA department, ACIO, or the *'Advanced Contact Intelligence Organization'*. Whether real or not, it is organizations such as these that fuel much of the speculation about 'the government within the government', the 'New World

Order' and other theories popular in the current culture of denial and secrecy.

After weighing up the available evidence, this new ultra-clandestine organization concluded that a race of extraterrestrials had arrived in the canyon and established some degree of contact with the natives. Since they had gone to the trouble of leaving a hidden store of information it was therefore considered worthwhile trying to decrypt the glyphs. The archaeological investigation suggested that the layout of the chambers was not random and it was possible that the information was also laid out in a specific manner, but there was no obvious way to decipher it. Fortunately, in one of the last chambers to be excavated, a small disc similar to a CD-rom was discovered. The disc was duly analyzed (by means unknown), but the researchers could not make sense of the information it contained. Regrettably, this lack of key information creates ripples of doubt concerning the story itself.

Two of the scientists involved on the project experienced a 'eureka' moment and concluded that they were approaching the problem the wrong way round and the disc would not decipher the drawings, the drawings were the key to the disc. The researchers approached their supervisors and requested permission to assemble a full-scale copy of the Ancient Arrow site in a laboratory. After some initial hesitation, due to both financial constraints this entailed and the lack of results so far, they were allowed to do so, but to divert suspicions the project was officially closed down, although, as with many covert projects, it continued as before. The continuing research revealed that the writings were similar to an ancient Sumerian text, and using this information they were able to decode the symbols in the paintings. When they did this information washed over them like a flood and they were able to design software to decode the thousands of pages of information stored on the disc. The outcome of all this activity was the discovery that the creators of the complex and the glyphs etc were a race calling themselves *'The Wingmakers'*. Astonishingly, they were not extraterrestrial, but, instead, were our descendants from centuries away in our far future, and crucially their message was one of peace.

Rightly or wrongly, one of the research team doubted that this heartening knowledge would ever reach the public, the only likely beneficiaries being the US Government and for obvious reasons the ever expanding arsenal of the military. The scientist, adopting the pseudonym, 'Dr. Anderson', stated that he was in regular touch with the Wingmakers themselves (although just how he did this is, once again, not revealed) and also stated that the Wingmakers were likewise observing the progress of the project and if the authorities failed to release the findings then they would. Annoyingly, but typically, just how the Wingmakers achieved their surveillance is not explained.

Dr Anderson approached his supervisors with his information and insisted that they share their findings with the public. The project director was furious and, after uttering dire threats at this show of conscience, promptly removed Anderson from the project. Anderson, quite wisely, disappeared from sight after making sure that information regarding the Wingmakers and their project reached a selection of journalists. It is still unknown if the project was eventually abandoned or still exists in the 'deep black', but whatever the outcome it has now effectively vanished from sight. Instinct suggests that, providing the project continued yielding information giving the US government a military or technological advantage, (although they are effectively one and the same) it would be mined until it ran dry, but only in conditions of the deepest secrecy and denial.

Will time travel ever become a reality or will it forever only exist in the equations of particle physicists, a tantalizing thought experiment like the famous puzzle of Schrödinger's Cat? Certainly, as we have seen, there are many claims that it is a reality, although, if so, it may be more likely in a non-physical sense. What to make of John Titor and the Wingmakers? An initial and reasonable reaction is to assume that they are an elaborate and intricate hoax, but for whose benefit? Are they just moneymaking scams (both the John Titor and the Wingmaker websites sold and continue to sell merchandise), or are they an attempt to reveal by 'drip feed' a great secret into the public domain? The Wingmakers supposedly traveled back to the eighth century AD to leave their time capsule, why? Why not travel to the here and now and presumably have their message found much more quickly rather than leave it for close on twelve hundred years? There is no obvious answer to this. As far as Aage Nost and Tony Bassett are concerned, Nost hosts a radio show in the USA and Bassett, who still lives in London, has faded into relative obscurity. Neither of them seems to have made much money from their enterprises, so why bother? Was this, to quote the artist Andy Warhol, their 'ten minutes of fame' perhaps? Sadly, the type of information they presented was more likely to earn them ridicule and notoriety than fame, so perhaps they did genuinely believe that they had perfected a method of reaching beyond the strictures of space and time.

The basic premise of time travel itself, although theoretically possible in the esoteric equations of quantum mechanics, is fraught with many pitfalls and anomalies. Logically, if a future race like the Wingmakers sent back this information for our, (and ultimately their) benefit, then we must have acted upon it and it must have worked. Or, conversely, our descendants are perhaps not happy with their lot and are attempting to change their present by persuading us to alter our future; paradox piled upon anomaly. If nothing else though, it is encouraging to think that mankind, as a species, has not managed to destroy itself and is still here on planet Earth. I'll leave the reader with this thought: what if the subterranean LHC in Switzerland really does eventually bring down the barriers of space-time and permit travel to and from the past and future, what then?

Chapter 32
Shadows on The Wall

Interdimensional visitors or Optical Illusions?

There have been many attempts to explain the possible existence of entities that sometimes appear in our reality. In many cases they have been called angels and demons, and, depending on the context and era, grays, reptilians and Nordics. In other words, these beings seem to have been with us in one form or another throughout recorded history, and whether regarded as emissaries of some deity or as the inhabitants of other star systems have left an indelible mark on the psyche of humanity. In more recent times however a new species of being has emerged and they are the enigmatic, mysterious and ephemeral 'Shadow People'. Of all the creatures that have appeared to human beings, these strange entities share much of their rationale with what are, by convention, deemed as ghosts, apparitions, spectres, demons and even extraterrestrials, which in this context refers to them in their literal sense, viz. not of this earth as opposed to the inhabitants of other planets.

While this is true to a degree there are clear differences: for example, ghosts etc. can be transparent, wispy images, or, equally, seemingly solid beings sharing all the attributes of humans. In addition they occasionally seem able to interact to the point of actually conversing with those who see them, and there are even reports that individuals have had physical contact, although this is extremely unusual. This at first seems something of a dichotomy, the physical being 'touched' by something that is by definition non-physical. Perhaps the sense of contact is induced in the mind of the person who is having the experience and might be similar to the tactile impressions experienced while dreaming? Or is the sensory experience invoked by whatever energy field is exuded by the entity? Sadly, this has to be left in the realms of speculation, as there is at present no effective way to measure or quantify experiences such as these.

Although the study of 'conventional' supernatural and paranormal phenomena is well documented, there is considerably less information concerning the aforementioned 'Shadow People', also known as *'Shadow Men'*, *'Shadow Folk'*, and in German as *'Schattenwesen'*. These unique entities, in terms of the alarm they produce in those who have fleetingly seen them, is second only to the infamous manifestations of so called 'poltergeist' phenomena (another German contribution to the lexicon of the supernatural). The Shadow People, although relatively recent in terms of modern folklore, are well known in the beliefs of the Native Americans whose legends mention them from the earliest times. When noticed, they appear as featureless, dark, shapes on the edge of the witnesses' vision, then, as if realizing that they have been spotted, quickly disintegrate or move rapidly to another area. There have been no recorded instances where they directly communicate with the witnesses, but they have been known to chase after, or on rare occasions physically attack the people who have seen them.

Multiple witnesses have on occasion observed the Shadow People and in every instance the observers have reported feelings of dread as if the entity was some sort of harbinger of doom. Whether their existence in the folklore of the Native American tribes is related to the fact that the tribes lived in simple dwellings illuminated by open fires and therefore more likely to produce shadows anyway is one factor to take into account. However, since this type of heat and light source was also ubiquitous in the more developed nations of mainland Europe prior to the colonization of America, one would expect similar accounts, but these do not seem to exist. Ghosts and spirits yes, but no Shadow People; one is then drawn to the question, what are they?

John Frum's Shadow

One curious parallel with the inhabitants of the Polynesian Islands lies in sightings of a character they named *'John Frum'*, a legendary being who appeared at around the same time the Second World War was raging. The name, 'John Frum', derives from the term, *'John from America'*, an oft-repeated phrase spoken by the US servicemen stationed there during the conflict in the Far East. This was in response to the innocent questions from the islanders when they asked who these strange warriors were and where they came from.

Rather than enter into conversations rendered difficult to near impossible by the lack of a common language other than Pidgin English, the servicemen overcame this by using a generic term understood by the local inhabitants, so John Frum was born. This fictional character became elevated almost to the level of a god who generously bestowed all sorts of wonderful gifts and trinkets upon the locals. Folding knives, torches, cans of food and soft drinks, fine fabrics, cigarettes and a thousand and one other items that we in the West take for granted. Perhaps more importantly, unlike the islanders who had little understanding of the subtleties of cause and effect, we are fully aware that these items do not just magically appear in the shops, they are designed, manufactured, distributed and have to be paid for – they are part of a developed society.

Not so with the relatively unsophisticated islanders who associated the items solely with the men and the flying machines and ships that they arrived in. Because of this, when the war finished and the men departed, the islanders created *'Cargo Cults''* venerating the men and their machines, and built small ships and aircraft out of wood along with wooden radio sets and the other paraphernalia associated with military bases hoping that the real items would be attracted by the 'lures'. This seems to be a variation on the practice of *'sympathetic magic'*, where small models or images are made of the person to be affected and imbued with characteristics of the real person in the hope that the wish, for good or ill, is made manifest in that person.

This is still true in the treatment of certain illnesses where a ribbon is tied round a tree branch or twig in the hope that the illness will transfer from the human being into the tree, or that the health of the tree (or bush) would somehow drive the illness from the human being. This of course ties into aspects of traditional herbal medicine where, for example, the bark of the willow tree was successfully used to treat minor aches and pains; modern research revealed no suggestion of any placebo effect either, because willow bark contains a substance present in the common painkiller, aspirin. Variations on this practice are still prevalent today where multinational pharmaceutical companies fund ethno-botanists and anthropologists etc. to seek substances and compounds in the medicinal plants and herbs used by remote jungle tribes. More importantly, returning to the Cargo Cults, glimpses of Frum were frequently seen in the flickering shadows around the islanders' village fires. From the contemporary descriptions Frum acted in a manner identical to the Shadow People, although due to the context it is not certain if he induced the same feelings of nascent panic. It may be reasonable to ask whether Frum was inadvertently created as a thought form by a shared craving to actualize the focus of their desire? Or, if not by accident, might the tribal shamans have had a hand in his 'birth' with their powerful invocations?

It appears that the creation of Frum also may also share a faint resonance with the so-called *'Philip Experiment'*; when, in 1972, members of the *'Toronto Society for Psychical Research'* led by George and Iris Owen decided to create an entity, which, prior to the attempt, they christened 'Philip'. The original experiments, which were suggestive of séances, were not successful, and it was not until they abandoned this approach and employed a more relaxed atmosphere that a measure of success was achieved. After three or four sessions of using the new method, a series of clearly audible sounds like knocks was heard coming from the table at which they sat. During further sessions the table levitated and moved around the room and the knocks would apparently respond to questions.

Although there is still much speculation about this project, it has been repeated several times since by a number of research groups and the results were remarkably similar. It is of course equally possible that the groups, rather than actually creating an entity from nothing, succeeded in opening a sort of 'portal' that allowed some curious being admission to our realm, which is not normally of good idea. It is important to realize that although the original 'Philip Experiment' was designed in the hope of inducing a collective hallucination, it may instead have demonstrated an example of *'psychokinesis'* (PK), or the ability to move items or induce sounds by non-physical means. Having said that, it does not explain the ability of the 'knocks' to respond correctly to questions. If this is the case, is it possible that these Shadow People are the unintentional and potentially malignant product of people dabbling with processes of which they have little understanding and even less control? A similar idea has been put forward to explain the existence of UFO's, and in particular their occupants.

Eyewitness accounts

As an investigator of the paranormal I have encountered a variety of strange phenomena, including what may well have been one of these Shadow People, and what follows is taken from a personal experience. During one case involving a series of quite dramatic hauntings, I visited the site, a small, old hotel, to interview the people who were encountering the haunting. After being shown around the building I was discussing the next stage of the investigation with the owner of the hotel (who was also the main witness). I was sitting facing her while she phoned her daughter who had also experienced some of the events, when suddenly my ears 'popped'. The feeling was identical to the physical reaction one experiences when an aircraft takes off and the cabin pressure changes. In spite of a blazing coal fire and the central heating (it was during the winter months) the temperature in the room abruptly dropped and, bizarrely, the quality of acoustics in the room changed, which is something I have noticed many times during a variety of cases.

My gaze was drawn to the wall behind the woman where I noticed a tall, dark shape forming. It looked human but with no detail and no features and as I watched it became increasingly dense. I blinked rapidly and glanced away but the dark shape remained. Not too sure of how to react I concentrated with all my being on mentally commanding it to leave, which it did, one second it was there and the next it had gone. With its disappearance the temperature in the room immediately rose and the sound quality, which had become slightly 'hollow', returned to normal. Everyone in the room had experienced a subtle change, although not everyone felt the same thing. If this was indeed a Shadow Person I can entirely empathize with other witnesses, for I experienced a quickly growing sense of unease while it was visible; no one else saw the figure although the rapid change in room temperature was commented upon. Intriguingly, there was one more incident during this case where I observed a hazy, featureless, black amorphous shape descend a short flight of stairs leading to attic bedrooms. It was the same flight of stairs that were at the epicenter of one of several manifestations in the hotel. In this instance the shape resembled a vertical cylinder approximately four feet high. Whether these were both examples of Shadow People is difficult to say with certainty, but they had most of the necessary attributes.

What are they?

These beings are reported to appear in two guises: one is a so-called *'hat man'*, a title given because in this example it appears to be wearing what looks like a fedora hat popular in the 1930's. The other and perhaps more common shape is the *'hooded figure'*, which pretty much describes what the outline looks like and when compared to my own experience seems to fit this particular profile precisely. Also reported are small, child like beings and sometimes shapeless masses that may assume a human outline and these outlines are mostly described as two-dimensional, although very rarely there are accounts where they seem to be three-dimensional. This also chimes with my second encounter on the staircase in the hotel. Although in all cases described as featureless, they are sometimes attributed with possessing red eyes; a feature consistent with accounts of the so-called 'Mothman'. As mentioned earlier, the people who have reported seeing them are sure that these entities are aware of their presence and, should they wish it, be capable of communication.

Although not generally noted for moving other than to vanish, where they have been seen to move it is in a very quick and jerky manner, and in addition, although the movements are unusually rapid, they seem to move in predetermined lines as if on tracks. This peculiar feature of their behaviour is perhaps highly significant. Is it possible that these entities have to move in accordance within extremely tight parameters in order to traverse the paths between their reality and ours? Might this be yet another hint relating to the mathematical underpinnings of the universe, the path into surrounding realties is a matter of exquisite precision relying on a knowledge of calculations, angles and degrees? It has already been conjectured that we carry in our heads the means to traverse the barriers separating us from these hidden dimensions. Is it only required to think of a specific equation and move in a certain manner to achieve the transition? Is this one of the secrets used by mages and sorcerers who employ specific forms of words and ritual movements in the operation of magic? The pieces all seem to point in one direction, but still no conclusive proof.

There is much speculation concerning the nature and point of origin of these entities, some people of a religious persuasion consider them to be demons while others regard them as a type of ghost. This is an interesting interpretation, which holds that their appearance, although apparently unlikely, is even less substantial than that of a ghost and is due to the fact that they may be the very last fading ember of a life that has ended, but for whatever reason cannot fully 'let go'. Perhaps so, but this does not fully gel with the impression that they are also somehow sentient and aware of the witnesses, unless of course our notion of consciousness and transient neurological states are wildly off the mark. It would also require a profound rethink in our ideas of how we pass to the afterlife, which is still mired in a morass of quasi-religious, half skeptical doubt and trepidation. It would also require that science and religion find some viable common ground not already hijacked by the learned bigots of both extremes professing absolute certainties both for and against the survival of consciousness after the body dies.

It is the fervent outpourings of these two entrenched groups that hinder and stifle serious research into this vital subject. One extreme ruthlessly demeans, ridicules, sneers at, and trivializes those brave enough to approach the subject with an open mind, while the other, although fully aware that there is an afterlife and that we eventually reach it, grimly explains away any serious independent research using its own template of superstition, doctrine and dogma. The result is that open-minded research that actually produces valid results is denied the oxygen of publicity for fear of upsetting the establishment. Perhaps this is best summed up using the old saying of, *"You can't fight city hall"*. Only that should now perhaps be altered to include, *"and the massed ranks of orthodoxy be it scientific or religious"*. Does it not seem strange that science continually shies away from disproving or contradicting what all religion is founded on? Perhaps not, because at our core we all have an atavistic need to believe in something greater than ourselves, but if so why shy away from proving it?

The Mechanism?

Another belief is that they are the inhabitants of alternate universes that very occasionally impinge on ours allowing them fleeting access. This idea has a variant suggesting that they exist directly in parallel with us but only allow glimpses of themselves at times of their own choosing. There is, perhaps typically, a school of thought suggesting they are in some way part of the UFO phenomenon and are related in some manner to the entities who pilot these craft. Equally it might be argued that as with some categories of 'visitor' and I use the term deliberately, they are time travelers, in effect they may be us. Before taking up some of these ideas it would be unfair to willfully ignore other more logical explanations such as the phenomenon of *'pareidolia'* where the brain can misinterpret random patterns of light and shade or shadows and textures and create familiar images such as faces and the human form.

This sometimes happens when an item of furniture in a poorly lit room is mistaken for a living person; perhaps this shares features with the common perceptual phenomenon of seeing 'faces in the fire'. There is also the neurological condition known as *'hypnogogia'*, which is experienced in the process of falling asleep (the same can happen while awakening and is called *'hypnopompia'*) allowing the experiencer to be awake but still 'see' images from their subconscious mind, rather like a waking dream. Perhaps the most telling effect of the condition is the feeling of dread that some people experience while having the experience, something that exactly mirrors the encounters with Shadow People. While plausible for some encounters what it does not do is explain the multiple sightings. There are also the effects reported by those who have consumed various non-prescription pharmaceuticals such as LSD, cocaine and amphetamines, which can also, in some instances, produce human shaped hallucinations. Quite typically we find that altered states of mind are the source of these sightings; what it does not tell us is whether the altered states of perception act as keys allowing these sightings to take place, or whether the visions are entirely spurious and artificial due to the action of the chemicals on the brain itself.

Yet another possibility is the action of external electromagnetic (EM) fields on the temporal lobes of the brain, something that had been exploited under test conditions by the previously mentioned Professor Michael Persinger at the Laurentian University in Ontario, Canada, whose work has already provided a tangible explanation for many of the phenomena encountered so far, but crucially not all. During the tests he conducted, some of the feelings and impressions were, in some cases, quite alarming and produced feelings of impending doom, an exact parallel with the Shadow People. It should be noted that the effects produced by artificial EM fields have also been encountered in naturally occurring areas of EM radiation where reports of paranormal events have frequently been reported.

While often used to demonstrate or insinuate that ghostly sightings may not genuine and purely the result of the brain reacting to external stimuli, debunkers and skeptics frequently claim that the visions of shamans and mystics who are under the effects of a variety of psychoactive substances are equally bogus. What the deniers and blinkered rationalists fail to realize is that the nature of consciousness is not fully understood and in all probability never will be, and specific drugs and EM fields may open unsuspected doorways in the mind permitting glimpses into hitherto uncharted and unexpected levels of reality.

There appears to be no consensus on the ethnicity, type or age of those who have seen the Shadow People, although the descriptions are remarkably similar within the known parameters of their appearance. There seems to be no prior ritual involved in their appearance, neither do they seem to be a channel for communication with the dead via the usual means of mediums and psychics. The only possibility regarding their nature seems to lie in a belief in the astral plain and the entities that allegedly exist there. Once again we are hampered by our vocabulary, or perhaps our lack of it, when discussing beings like the Shadow People; it is an identical situation to that encountered when dealing with almost any aspect of the paranormal and how it relates to the *'spirit world'*.

The use of the term, *spirit world,* which I have italicized deliberately, is both regrettable and unfortunate because it is encumbered by the redundant baggage surrounding the uneasy memory of the charlatans and cynics who subverted it for their own ends, usually financial. I have kept them quite separate from the merely deluded who acted in good faith and gave messages of comfort that originated entirely in their own subconscious minds; they were wrong but relatively harmless. There is, however, a quite separate type of communicator whose talent lies entirely within the right hand side of their brain, in the creative, instinctive and artistic mass of neurons, electrical charges and chemicals that is the antithesis of the logical, sensible, calculating, left brain. It is the ability of those fortunate enough to be able to disengage the left and right sections of the brain and retune their minds to what lies alongside us displaying its existence under our very noses. This, I am sure, is the domain of the Shadow People; it is likely that those who see them have experienced a few seconds of clarity when, for whatever reason, their right brain perceived an unfiltered glimpse of what is there around us.

There is just one more possibility that involves one more

paradigm shift in our thinking and it is that these dark, menacing, ephemeral Shadow People might just be the reverse of the entities known as the *'Beings of Light'*. To be sure there is much in the New Age movement to suggest that we are creatures of light and that light is fundamental to our existence, which of course in terms of sunlight it is. Although this might at first sight seem rather unlikely, as the ancient alchemical truism says, *'as above, so below'*; and so it is, for everything, irrespective of what or where it is, there is an opposite. This is in the law of natural balance, Yin and Yang, high and low, salt and sweet, kind and cruel, love and hate, and light and dark; it is also reflected in a line from The Lord's Prayer, viz. *'On Earth as it is in Heaven'*. It is not clear whether this particular allusion was intended, but nevertheless it is there for those with the eyes to see.

Whether or not this is the case, I cannot be certain, but it makes sense, although why the opposite of these beings of light (if that is what they are) should emanate an aura of malice is a matter of opinion. What would happen if these beings of light and darkness were to meet, might the reaction be the same as is predicted for that of matter and anti-matter – the utter annihilation of both in a fearsome explosion? Perhaps it is better that we do not know and just accept their existence for what it is, an enigma that has no ready answer. While they may well have some basis in reality, equally they may be a figment created by defects in our psychology and physiology and there are persuasive and powerful arguments for both points of view. However, in the end the judges will be those who have encountered and still encounter these remote and apparently unfriendly beings. Unfortunately, until we do find a rationale to explain their existence they must remain in the lost universe of their cousins, the ghosts and specters that have been with us since the beginning of time.

Chapter 33
'Children of the Gods'

This chapter deals with one aspect of the New Age that is riddled with thought processes running contrary to convention and possibly on a collision course with standard spiritual belief; it also resonates with some of the strands predicted by science fiction writers. While I hold no particular views on the subject of the so-called *'Indigo Children'*, *'Crystalline Children'*, the *'Super Psychic Chinese Children'* and the rather disconcertingly named, *'Children of Aids'*, they have apparently caught both the attention and imagination of a relatively large number of people within the New Age and UFO movements, and as such are worthy of serious consideration.

Both of these subjects provide fertile ground for the damned to occupy, but since I keep an open mind on all areas of the paranormal I can accept the rationale behind their existence, although as an investigator I cannot accept this without challenge. For this reason, although I shall present the reader with evidence, both pro and con, I have attempted to remain neutral and leave you to decide for yourselves whether the phenomenon is genuine or only present in the imaginations of the parents of the children and the people who originally popularized the notion. We will first consider what is perhaps the most widespread example of this recent phenomenon, i.e. the 'Indigo Children'.

The Indigo Children

Imagine if you will the unnatural emotional situation faced by any normal human mother (or indeed father) of yielding up the satisfaction, comfort, joy and fulfillment of parenthood to the rather queasy feeling that their child is not entirely human and may, to all intents and purposes, be non-terrestrial. Such is one of the more extreme scenarios faced by those who have accepted that their offspring belong to the so-called *'Indigo Children'*, babies that, although born naturally of human parents, are credited with being children of the stars. Their parents are relegated to little more than surrogates charged with their earthly welfare and upbringing until such times as they are able to look after themselves.

The children unfailingly appear to possess exotic talents and abilities, chief among these is the facility to channel information from their real (non human) 'parents' coupled to a range of psychic powers including healing and natural telepathy. In some ways they are reminiscent of the unearthly children featured in John Wyndham's excellent book, *'The Midwich Cuckoos'*, which was later adapted for the screen as a series of films beginning with *'Village of The Damned'*, (1960, Dir. Wolf Rilla), although so far their mission, if that is what it is, unlike that of the children of Midwich is apparently benign. It should be made clear that in some cases where these children have been identified the parents seem quick to advertise if not actually exploit the situation.

All this may be so, but a word of caution, it might be reasonable to wonder if, in such cases, the parents are attempting to fit a template of their own design onto the instinctive actions, words and possibly neurological condition of their child. A less extreme interpretation of Indigo Children views them as bricks in a spiritual wall designed to bring about a sea change in human evolution, a claim not uncommon in the New Age paradigm. Their 'talents' in this version of the story tend to involve enhanced empathy and often creativity, admittedly two attributes that are badly needed in the self-centred, hedonistic, divisive and largely compassionless society in which we live. The trouble is, if the child is encouraged to accept that they are in some way special, whether they are or not, they will quite naturally come to believe it is so; this is something we will look at later.

It should be noted that these children are not described as being 'Indigo' because they are colored blue, but rather because they were named 'Indigos' by Nancy Ann Tappe, a 'synesthete' and psychic, who first coined the term in her 1982 book, *'Understanding Your Life Through Color'*. Chief among her claims was that she could discern the aura, (or nebulous cocoon of 'life energy', roughly analogous to the electromagnetic field that is emitted by any functioning electrical device), that allegedly surrounds each and every one of us. The condition of synesthesia is a relatively harmless neurological dysfunction causing the sufferer to 'see' or perceive sounds as colors and vice versa, in effect the internal 'wiring' of the brain is not 100% correct. A similar phenomenon was regularly reported, particularly in the 1960's, by users of psychoactive substances like LSD, who regularly described 'seeing the sounds' and 'listening to the pretty colors' while under the effects of the drug. According to Ms Tappe, she began to notice a preponderance of children possessing indigo auras during the late 1970's and currently estimates that approximately 60% people aged between 14 and 25 are indigo. More significant is her remarkable assertion that 97% of pre-teen children are also Indigo.

It is a well to consider at this point that claims of individuals who are (or were) here on Earth to assist in a spiritual revolution are not new and many iconic and inspirational figures such as Christ, Mohammed, Abraham, Buddha, Osiris, Tammuz and many other spiritual leaders were sent to save the human race from its own failings. All of them, according to the era and society they lived in, were able to convert huge numbers of people to their cause and indeed the majority still command disciples and believers numbering in their tens of millions. It has to be noted that there still are a number of people who claim to be messiahs and with varying degrees of success attempt to lead their bands of followers to 'salvation'. Sadly, many of them appear to be cult leaders more interested in manipulating their flock for their own ends. Cults aside, this all sounds rather like a variant on Prof. Rupert Sheldrake's theory of *'Morphogenetic Fields'* using the by now almost standard example of *'The Hundredth Monkey Syndrome'*, a concept which, broadly speaking, means that the more people who come to accept a new idea or practice, the more people are likely to display the same practice whether they consciously learn it or not. In other words, according Prof. Sheldrake an invisible field of 'information energy' surrounds us, that in the right conditions percolates into us almost by a type of osmosis, or more correctly we inadvertently receive it like a radio or TV set.

According to the theory, as the numbers grow we assimilate the knowledge/information with increasing speed until a 'tipping point' is reached and we as a race become as one, a gigantic gestalt being. If this is true then we might not necessarily benefit from such a 'gift', because it may serve agendas that are not in the best interests of the human race; like mind control. One is also tempted to draw comparisons with the concept of 'memes', or the proposition that certain good ideas, particularly ones that have a direct benefit on the individual and society in general, actually perpetuate themselves almost as if they had sentience. This of course is a difficult type of logic to follow; it is rather like saying that a thermostat has intelligence because it performs a mechanical function in response to an increase or decrease in temperature, a conclusion that is tenuous at best.

Although the concept of these supposedly unique children was invented by Ms Tappe, it achieved a place of prominence in the New Age psyche in the book, *'The Indigo Children: The New Kids Have Arrived'*, written in 1998 by Jan Tober and Lee Carroll. The source of the subject matter of this work was channeled from an entity called *'Kyron'*, evidently one of the ranks of the so-called 'Ascended Masters'. According to Carroll and Tober, a married couple, when talking about their book in the wider community they tend not to mention the source of the information it contains, as, not surprisingly, they do not believe the potential audience and market for the book outside the New Age community would readily accept its validity.

Among the many traits associated with these children is a tendency to antisocial behaviour unless they are mixing with their peers; as a result of this their schooling is problematic. Added to this is their rejection of authority and an elevated sense of self-importance; another two factors that are less than conducive to conventional education. A less sympathetic and more pragmatic interpretation of these traits views these children as suffering from *Attention Deficit Hyperactive Disorder* (ADHD), *Obsessive-Compulsive Disorder* (OCD) and/or *Autism*. In most of these instances the conditions are treated using a range of drugs, but chiefly 'Ritalin', which is a type of amphetamine. However, a more conspiratorial mind may interpret this situation as the deliberate use of a 'chemical cosh' to subdue their development and prevent them developing their full potential, whatever that may be.

Undoubtedly the way many of these youngsters behave can be highly disruptive within a household and a cause of extreme frustration to their parents. One has to wonder how those that are convinced of their children's 'specialness' and are to be encouraged in what they do manage to maintain a degree of control over them. Or perhaps ADHD, OCD and Autism are subtly different from the tantrums and traumas exhibited by these Indigo Children. It has been suggested that parents who decide that their child is Indigo may actually cause harm to them by failing to recognize the previously mentioned conditions; but perhaps more cautiously this is connected to the insidious methods used to prevent their development and eventual flowering. As hinted at earlier, is it possible that we are actually creating a new breed of evolved being because we want it to happen? Are the desires of those parents who choose to see their offspring as special and different actually bringing this about in some manner by causing the child to become what they imagine they should be, and if so is it within the gift of humanity to think these beings into existence? If this is the case then surely it would be much simpler to excise evil and injustice from society by simply wishing it away in the first place? But perhaps not, maybe this is an oversimplification and there needs to be another agency involved.

Another issue to be addressed is the admitted fact that, as with the observations of Ms Tappe, there has indeed in recent years been a rapid increase in children diagnosed with ADHD etc., but this has been attributed to many factors including the increasing level of toxins that surround us plus the large number of synthetic ingredients in the food that we eat. Or, is it possible that the change in diet has actually altered the genetic code of some children for the better; are we witnessing a new and benign genesis of the human race? It has also been suggested that the Indigo's tend to have poor sleep patterns and often stay awake for hours on end, only succumbing when they are literally out on their feet; and, as already mentioned, they apparently possess paranormal abilities and heightened awareness. This should come as no real surprise, because there is at least one valid reason for it; the longer the brain is deprived of sleep, the greater the build up of serotonin, which is one of several powerful neuro-transmitters mediated by sleep. It may be the reason why ghosts, phantoms and ET's are most often seen at night when levels are at their highest. Perhaps the neurology of Indigo's is 'retuned' by elevated levels of serotonin permitting them access to impressions denied to the rest of us. This link leads us to yet another example of this phenomenon, the so-called 'Crystalline Children'.

The Clouded Crystal

Another manifestation of the desire to rise above our current level of human existence is the claimed appearance of another subgroup within the human species, that of the *'Crystalline Children'*, who display most and possibly more of the attributes ascribed to the Indigo's. This information arrives, once again, from the dubious and entirely unverifiable source of the 'Ascended Masters', and as previously mentioned with the Indigo's they are not entirely comfortable in the presence of any but their peers. Among their alleged talents is the ability see beyond the three dimensions, and possibly four, assuming that time is a dimension, that govern our physical existence. They are, according to what is currently known about them, evidently attuned with the frequencies of light and it is hinted that they are, or will be, once fully developed, almost godlike in their abilities and bring with them truths that have become either lost or distorted beyond recognition over millions of years of human evolution.

Their DNA is in some way reprogrammed and in effect 'blueprinted', so that it is exactly as our progenitors intended. Their purpose is the re-harmonization of the human race so that it resonates with 'The One', another reference to the gestalt that may, or may not, represent Cosmic Consciousness – in other words a reinterpretation of the Eastern mantra that *'all is one'* and the ancient Alchemical and Mystery School teaching of *'as above, so below'*. In truth, these ostensibly 'new' belief systems are little more than retreads of aeons old wisdom and teachings and may be (more cynically) merely a moneymaking platform for the new gurus. All of this assumes that, as we have seen, we are the product, not of natural selection, but of a deliberate and sustained act designed to produce the human race. Not that there is anything fundamentally wrong with this concept, it's just that it is far from new.

The Crystalline Variant on this theme seems to rely on the

idea that we are in fact, each and every one of us, a tiny fragment of the whole, a miniscule version of the entire entity and these children will cause us to reunite into the totality (gestalt again?) that surrounds us. It also relies on the nature and understanding of the DNA that makes us what we are and how, as it alters, allows us a means of interdimensional access to higher communication. It stops short of actually saying, although heavily implies, that we might eventually communicate with our creator(s) on some exotic level of existence. What it does not say is whether the DNA of the animals who also live on the Earth might also evolve into higher states of consciousness, particularly certain species of aquatic mammals like whales and dolphins that already appear to have a well-developed degree of communication, intelligence and awareness. We should not lose sight of the fact that this information allegedly derives from already advanced creatures currently existing without a fixed shape within a light matrix. While the advent of crystalline children may be a little too much to fully accept, perhaps we can more easily understand another two alleged strands of emerging super-humanity, the super psychic children of China and the children who cannot become ill.

Reprogramming the Helix

Although perhaps the most interesting of all these alleged 'new humans' are the children who do not become ill, we should first look briefly at the so-called *'Super Psychic Children of China'*. According the evidence, such as it is, they were first noted circa 1984, the same era as that of the emergence of the Indigo Children. Evidently the Chinese government identified one such child who scored way off the scale during a standard psi experiment designed to measure paranormal abilities. Following this discovery and the attention it drew, other parents started noticing odd 'talents' and behaviour in their own children until the numbers spiraled into the many hundreds. Every test devised to test them revealed telepathic and precognitive abilities that went well above chance and in most cases the children tested scored 100% irrespective of how the test was conducted.

Another of their claimed talents is the curious ability to read without using their eyes, in other words they were able to 'read' words and colors using other parts of their anatomy such as their fingers, ears, and patches of skin on their arms and chests. Although a remarkable discovery, if true, and in spite of the exited announcements, it is not entirely unique, as, over the years, this particular aptitude has been noted among various people. One in particular was Mollie Fancher, a woman who lived in America in the late 19th century. Blind and crippled due to a childhood accident she exhibited the capability of selecting by touch alone various colors of thread used in embroidery from a box located above her bed. Although not a Roman Catholic she also occasionally exhibited traditional signs of the stigmata, which drew some considerable comment.

She also displayed manifestations of multiple personality disorder where she exhibited at least two distinct personalities beside her own. In addition she was reputedly both psychic and to some extent telepathic, this raises the question of whether she may have been a precursor of the superchild revolution. It certainly gives reason to question whether many people who have been consigned to psychiatric care were in fact only demonstrating aspects of their superhuman potential and not signs of mental illness. It is strange that depending on the mores and customs of individual societies, some of them regard the mentally disturbed to be some way 'gifted' and worthy of veneration, considering them to be communing with the gods. Is this perhaps yet another example of the involuntary recognition of a coming super race caused by genetic information bleed-through from the pre-existing program? If this is the case the strange talents shown by Mollie and many others over the years may well have been slight defects in the timing of the inbuilt genetic clock determining our elevation to another level of existence. The next group we consider holds the prospect of near immortality for the human race; they are the *'Children of AIDS'*.

Chapter 34
The Children of AIDS

This truly remarkable evolutionary development first came to light, again at around the same time as the other two groups, in the late 1970's early 1980's, when a child was born that already was infected with the deadly condition of **A**cquired **I**mmune **D**eficiency **S**yndrome, now known simply as **AIDS**, and a prime candidate for damnation from the evangelical right wing if ever there was one. As is now known, this condition renders the patient unable to fight off ordinary infections that in normal people the immune system deals with automatically by destroying any invading foreign organism. The child was tested at six months old and was indeed still infected as it was a year later; then something remarkable happened. The child, a boy, was left until he was six years old and tested again when, miraculously, he was AIDS free. Naturally the tests were repeated and proved identical; there was no trace of AIDS whatsoever, or indeed of HIV, which is the precursor of full blown AIDS.

Following this remarkable development, the boy was taken to UCLA where he was exposed to a series of tests to examine his DNA for any abnormalities; these tests revealed that the child did not have normal, standard, human DNA. Although this is an extremely complex subject I have attempted to explain it in terms that are accessible. This is slightly daunting but vital because of what may be happening to us. In the normal, human, genetic code there is a set of instructions defining what we are. Among these are units comprising three nucleotides representing one amino acid, they are called *'codons'*. We as human beings possess sixty-four of these codons, of which only twenty-three are used, twenty are turned on and the other three act as start (initiation) and stop (termination) switches controlling the rest, rather like the digital switching arrangements used in a computer. This is an analogy that works well and is something that we will return to shortly. The unused 'codons' have always been assumed to be part and parcel of our so-called 'Junk DNA', something that we no longer require in our evolutionary process, although this was apparently not the case with this child because he had twenty-four of these codons switched on. Following this discovery his DNA was tested again to see just how resistant to disease it actually was and the results were truly breathtaking.

The scientists exposed his blood cells to a progressively stronger dose of AIDS and it was not until the dosage was in the order of thousands of times stronger that his blood cells were damaged. The same experiment was tried using a range of other diseases including various types of cancer and his blood did not react or succumb to any of them, he appeared to be immune to all diseases. Following this discovery a clandestine program was instituted to examine blood cells from a wide range of children from all ethnic groups and social classes and much to the surprise of the scientists they found that the altered DNA was not by any means unique to one child.

The numbers ran into tens of thousands; something was definitely happening, something wonderful yet at the same time frightening. The question then was how and why? The implication here is that, as with the Indigo's, the greater the number the more quickly the change spreads. The method by which this occurs is, however, highly speculative, as is the evidence itself, unless of course 'they', the faceless, ruling *'ubermensch'*, really are behind a monstrous cover-up and, for a variety of reasons both political and economic, are denying this information to the general public. It is certain that the multinational manufacturers in the pharmaceutical industry would be less than pleased to see their highly lucrative market vanish almost overnight and as such would go to any lengths to stop this from happening.

According to what knowledge there is, whether suppressed or not, the mechanism behind the change seems to be largely internal. All that is required, apparently, is a strong enough desire to make the change to one's DNA and it will happen; the use of meditation techniques seem to be an advantage though. In fact what this sounds like is a variant on Chaos Magic, where a wish or desire becomes a reality at the quantum level and, providing this has been done correctly, manifests a physical change in the real world. On other levels there is a clear reference to the power of positive thinking where a person who is ill is encouraged to think in a positive manner, which does seem to have an effect on the speed of recovery. What is uncertain is how the original and initial change was made; for unless there was a series of lucky accidents, then the first people to display these genetic peculiarities had to be given outside help, unless our DNA has always carried the message as part of its internal programming. While considering this, it is important to realize that the information controlling our genes and how they function is not entirely stored in the genetic code. The additional information is contained, rather like computer sub-routines, in regulatory sequences, intergenetic segments and areas devoted to the structure of chromosomes, which brings us back to the link with computers.

As previously mentioned, the codons and additional elements in the gene pattern that switch the rest of the DNA on and off act like timers in a standard digital computer or programmable logic controller: no matter how clever or fleeting, they are either on or off with no halfway position. The only way to improve on this situation in computers is to use dual and quad-core processors so that they can multi-task more easily. This is a development from the original method of using separate sub-processors to deal with the more mundane tasks like number crunching. Staying with the computer analogy there is, however, another method currently under development and that is in the esoteric field of 'quantum computing'. This near magical infant science relies on the 'uncertainty principle', which posits that the state of any subatomic particle cannot be predicted at any given time and they exist in an infinite number of states. It is this previously unsuspected property that should eventually result in a type of computer that will operate in a number of modes at any one time and as such can carry out a near limitless number of functions simultaneously. The components used in the processing are still electronic, but they are now operating in applications that their inventors could not have imagined.

As we have seen, the method by which these electronic devices function has many parallels with the science of genetics and provides a good comparison. Both rely on programming to function and both are capable of being reprogrammed to produce different effects. The difference is, so far, that unlike the application of computers, any alterations to the genetic code have, in the main, been confined to what amounts to tinkering around the edges of its vast potential. The restraints on development have in the main been ethical and/or religious, where the very thought of tinkering with the human genome is likened to interfering with God's work, which, in fundamentalist circles is absolute anathema irrespective of how beneficial it might be. While there is undoubtedly an official ban on some aspects of this research, it would be interesting to discover what work is currently conducted under the cloak of 'black projects'. Although these developments fall well short of explaining the incredible complexity of inducing changes in specific elements of the genetic code to permit evolutionary leaps, nevertheless it is allegedly occurring at an ever-increasing rate. One can only ponder and speculate on what might occur if more of these codons were switched on; we can only hope that we are ready for the change and recognize it when it happens.

Conclusion

Is this all feasible or is it not? As we have seen, the youngsters called Indigo Children and/or Crystal Children are indeed an enigma. Are they a natural progression in human development triggered through some predetermined change in the human genome, or are they the inadvertent result of the increasingly toxic environment in which we live? Is this some type of corroboration of the Gaia hypothesis showing that the planet on which we live is indeed to some extent sentient and is attempting to alter us, it's children, in order to save itself. Or are the Indigo's and all the rest no more than a fantasy created by over imaginative and over protective parents determined to believe that their children are not in some way 'damaged', but reject it by submerging themselves in the fantasy that they are instead 'gifted'.

The purpose of these supposed evolved beings is nothing less than the redemption of the human race, a noble cause that no one would argue with, except that, as we have seen, this is really nothing new, only the packaging is different. *'The Space Brothers', 'The Council of Nine' 'The Ascended Masters', 'The Secret Chiefs'* and now 'gifted children', be they indigo, crystal, psychic or 'reprogrammed', there is no difference. A more cynical view is that this situation is entirely artificial and manmade, yet another symptom of the frantic and dizzy society in which we live. It is strange that as our rejection of organized religion gains momentum, we still apparently need something to cling to and so we invent one. We have seen this in the past with the advent of Ufology, which was perhaps at its zenith from the 1950's until the late 1980's. From personal experience I have seen this amply demonstrated during public meetings and conferences devoted to the study of strange phenomena, be it UFO's, hauntings or whatever. The intense, almost devout look on the faces of people in the audience, had the look and feel of a church congregation with the need to make sense of the world, but in a manner that best appealed to those attending. But instead of a God it was an extraterrestrial, which, I suppose, is what precisely what God is, a being that lives without the constraints of time and space, that is both omniscient and omnipotent, although, sadly, as with ET, God seems equally elusive. If these children are the next step, then we are truly favored that the process has begun and we may yet rise out of the mire that traps us. Ultimately in matters not whether the message comes via Ascended Masters, Space Brothers or Indigo Children, if the message is valid then it has to emerge one way or another. We must hope that they do not regard us as inferior and take steps to cleanse our memory from the face of the planet, to remove all trace of us from the gene pool. If this process can self-start then we must hope that the next stage, whatever that might be, continues to improve us as a species and we achieve the destiny prewritten for us in the coding of our DNA. There are indeed interesting times ahead.

Chapter 35
Implant

A re-evaluation of the alien implant phenomenon

Although the subject of alien implants seems like an open and shut case to the UFO community, it is not, and here the reader is presented with a viable alternative. This is not to say that implantation does not occur, for it almost certainly does, but, and here is the great heresy, perhaps not from an extraterrestrial source. In this chapter we will examine the process of brainwashing and other techniques used to subjugate and control people. This is not pleasant, but then again neither are people who do it, especially those who are blinkered by the notion that what they do is in the best interests of their country, or the scientists whose motivations are solely those of self-interest and financial gain. Who knows, perhaps the 'aliens' are more inhuman and closer than we think.

Almost from the beginning of modern Ufology, which, to all intents and purposes began circa 1947, the rather off-putting phenomenon of so-called 'alien implants' has emerged. These bizarre artefacts are sometimes discovered by accident during unrelated medical procedures involving X-ray's and MRI scans under the skin of those unfortunate enough to have been allegedly abducted by the occupants of extraterrestrial vehicles. They have been located in almost every part of the human body, including inside the skull and nasal cavities, in the webbing between the fingers and toes, and other, mainly fleshy, areas. They are, with the possible exception of inside the skull, not especially deep and can normally be detected by touch alone.

Their purpose is, even after many decades, a matter for conjecture, but it is normally assumed to be for the purpose of monitoring the location and/or physiology of the person into whom they have been inserted. They have been ascribed other functions too, including establishing the composition and molecular structure of the host body in which they are carried, monitoring the function of the nervous system and perhaps even observing the aging process. Alternatively, it is speculated that they are used to control and otherwise manipulate the host body. There have been a few reports of the removal of these implants by those who originally inserted them, i.e. the 'aliens' removed them after they had served their purpose; but most often they have been removed using standard operating techniques by surgeons here on Earth.

One of these surgeons is Dr Roger Leir, who claims that his medical team has removed more than a dozen items of allegedly non-earthly origin. Dr Leir claims that following evaluation in laboratories such as The Los Alamos National Laboratory (LNAL) in Albuquerque, New Mexico, the objects do not conform to terrestrial scientific knowledge and show various chemical bonds not found in conventional science. Dr Leir's team has also detected an extremely thin membrane around these objects, a membrane composed of elements and tissue taken from the body of the person from whom it was removed. It has been suggested that if a technique such as this was duplicated by terrestrial science it would solve many problems related to organ rejection found in transplant surgery. However this 'protective membrane' is exactly what the human body would produce to protect itself to from a foreign, although not necessarily 'alien' in the sense of extraterrestrial, invader. Precisely how these artefacts function and their source of power is not currently known, but it may be that, if genuine, they use and/or convert the tiny voltages found in the human body. Another possibility exists that they might be passive devices and function like the security chips sometimes located on motor cycles and, more commonly, in animals. These operate by responding to the signals from an external scanner. This is quite different from the active transponders fitted to security vans that carry large sums of cash and valuables.

However, some of these artefacts – and not just those found by Dr Leir – when analyzed, have proved rather unremarkable in composition and were found to consist of small pellets of compacted tissue and fatty deposits, and even those that were made of other materials like glass and metal shards are assumed to have punctured the skin accidentally e.g. during accidents etc. Interestingly, in all cases there were no indications of how they were inserted into the host body. Perhaps they were initially too deep to notice and the entry site healed over naturally, but over time they slowly percolated towards the surface of the skin: there are many valid, conventional reasons to explain their presence.

On the other hand, items have been removed from supposed 'abductees' that bear a striking resemblance to contemporary microcircuits and other items that we can readily recognize as some kind of electronic hardware, (albeit very small). These are clearly different from the other, perhaps natural items, but still a hard core of believers insist that the use of organic material is merely a disguise to make them appear this way. As with the obviously recognizable manufactured items, it has even been speculated that they are currently dormant, simply awaiting a signal to begin functioning. Not surprisingly Dr Leir is certain that these objects are not terrestrial and provide evidence of alien abduction.

Another well-known UFO researcher and investigator, Mr Derrel Simms, actively promotes the concept of alien implants and claims to possess a number of these objects that have also been surgically removed from various people. Although Mr Simms travels the world giving presentations on this subject to UFO and related conferences, when approached by a TV company that was making a documentary about this particular phenomenon, although happy to allow inspection, he refused to permit any of these objects to be taken for independent analysis. Under the circumstances it is difficult to blame him, but it is nonetheless unfortunate as his steadfast refusal does not exactly reinforce the case for their authenticity. As already stated, some of these objects are clearly artificial and if they were removed from otherwise normal human beings who had been 'abducted', then perhaps we should look more closely at their assumed function.

It is logical that if they were implanted by a non-terrestrial race then the beings who implanted them might well require detailed information about how the physiology of human beings functions. It would also make sense if the non-terrestrials wanted to obtain a working knowledge of human brain function – hence the implantation of these objects in the nasal cavities and inside the skull, although skull implants of this type are extremely rare. The implantation process does cause one to ask some pertinent questions though, especially if these races are presumably continuing with their implantation program. It also leads one to wonder if there are a number of non-earthly races with their own information gathering agendas, or is there is some sort of 'galactic data-bank' where information such as this is stored and shared? Judging by the apparently indiscriminate choice of implantation subjects and despite the claims of 'repeat abductees', it appears that selection is on a continuing, arbitrary and entirely *ad hoc* basis.

Although the collection of information appears to be fairly focused on human beings, why should this be the case? Is it possible that these 'implants' might also be found in the animal kingdom? This question is more logical than it might at first appear, especially in view of the number of so-called 'cattle mutilations' where individual animals are singled out for what appear to be specific veterinary/surgical procedures. As far as I am aware, the investigations into these events have concentrated on the actual wounds and the organs removed; it is unknown whether any heed was paid to whether or not any implants were discovered. If any non-earthly monitoring was indeed carried out, it would, once again, be in the interests of those conducting this work to examine the physiology of various species, unless of course all this has already been done – after all who would know, and the animals are certainly not going to say.

Mind Control and Brainwashing

So, there we have a case for implants based entirely on the assumption that they are carried out by races not native to this planet, or perhaps even this universe; but if not as part of an unknown program managed by non-terrestrial beings, then who? Is it possible that these implants are part of an experiment that is of entirely terrestrial origin and orchestrated by the intelligence services of various powers around the world. Let's look at the evidence, and in doing so we must not lose sight of the proven fact that intelligence agencies, especially in the United States of America and Russia, have used the hype surrounding the hypothesis that alien spacecraft visit this planet. They have repeatedly done this to good effect in disinformation campaigns designed to conceal their own clandestine projects and cast ridicule on anyone providing perhaps genuine information. This cynical response is entirely based on the desire to conceal any military advantage from the eyes of enemies and rivals, or, conversely, hide it in plain sight.

Part of this process may have been the development of a variety of devices designed to provide information about specific people and more worryingly to induce specific responses in them by remote control. In order to understand this policy, which is not a work of the imagination, we have to look at some truly horrendous procedures carried out on human beings in the name of 'national security' and 'progress'. Perhaps its most recent incarnation is the much vaunted 'war against terror', the results of which are seen all around us, especially with the rapid increase in the loss of personal liberty. Many slightly older people will remember the original version of a film entitled *'The Manchurian Candidate'*, which was first released in 1962 and directed by John Frankenheimer. This film is set just after the 1948 Korean War and concerns an attempt by the North Koreans to assassinate a US politician using a 'programmed' former American POW. The methods used to achieve this ranged from the brutal to the highly sophisticated, but mainly relied on the tried and tested methods of long term disorientation, hypnosis and narcotic drugs. At that time, the height of the lengthy, insidious and unrelenting 'cold war', the concept of mind control was known simply as 'Brainwashing'.

The term, 'Brainwashing', was first conceived by a journalist named Edward Hunter and originally appeared in print in a 1950's article that appeared in the 'Miami News'. The name of the technique, which seems to have been developed into its present form by the Sino/Soviet axis, comes from the Chinese words *'hsi-nao'* or to 'cleanse the mind'. Prior to this, these words had no sinister overtones. The concept and viability of brainwashing came to a head during aforementioned Korean War when the Chinese were determined to make captured US pilots confess to a range of 'crimes', including the use of ordinance containing chemical weapons and toxins. Curiously enough, these displays of political point scoring mostly involved US combatants in this conflict. The original methods of 'brainwashing' involved prolonged solitary confinement, complete isolation from outside stimuli, and sleep deprivation. Of course brutalizing and punishing prisoners is nothing new and has occurred in various forms since time began, the difference here is rather than purely designed to gather information by any means possible or mete out random brutality, this was a method to 're-educate' individuals for political and propaganda purposes.

The subject was constantly pressurized, humiliated and

controlled in their every thought, word and deed, and after approximately six weeks was judged sufficiently 'softened up' to progress to the next stage. These 'stages' continued until the victim suddenly realized that the only way to get out was to unconditionally believe whatever they were told and act on it. The techniques were quickly absorbed and adapted by the Americans who thought that this process, which could take many months, might be speeded up and from this was born the decision taken in 1953 by Allen Dulles, the then head of the CIA, to 'improve' on the techniques. This fateful choice started a course of action beginning with PROJECT ARTICHOKE through MK-DELTA and culminating in the excesses of the notorious MK-ULTRA.

Much of the experimentation in this evolutionary process involved the services of a Scots born Canadian psychiatrist called Dr. Ewan Cameron and took place outside the USA, which officially could not countenance such experimental medical skulduggery, in *'The Allan Memorial Institute'* in Montreal, Canada. The methods employed by Cameron included a process called 'depatterning', which involved repeated electroshocks, the same as those involved in electro-convulsive therapy (ECT), coupled with extended drug induced sleep of up to thirty days and sometimes considerably more, with the later added 'refinements' of the hallucinogen LSD and the paralyzing drug, curare, to ensure the patient remained motionless. Such was his desire to achieve results that the level of the ECT, the number of applications and the dosage of the drugs used by Cameron and his team were many times above the normal limits. Before continuing, it is as well to consider that the US government still transports suitable candidates for experimentation and of course questioning to 'torture friendly' countries such as Algeria, Cuba and Poland, where robust methods of interrogation that can be applied still continue today, especially in the wake of 9-11. Is this immoral and unethical when one factors in the mayhem that the organizations these individuals work for actually inflict on the world?

It is important to realize that Cameron was no second-rate charlatan. He was the first president of the *'World Psychiatric Association'* and considered eminent in his field. One must therefore ask why a well respected and ostensibly benevolent man such as this, who had taken the Hippocratic Oath, would link his work to the clandestine machinations of groups like the CIA, who, incidentally, also funded Cameron's research to the tune of tens of thousands of dollars every year. The reason why may lie either in his misguided belief that he was 'helping' his patients and the additional research opportunities and funding supplied by the CIA was therefore welcome, or the even more dubious motive, that he was acting for the previously mentioned 'greater good' and benefiting the interests of national security in the process. The net result of this odious research reduced the unfortunate recipient to an almost vegetative and unresponsive state.

Following 'depatterning', Cameron then began a process he called 'psychic driving', which involved bombarding the patient/victim with repeated messages through 'pillow speakers' as they lay in bed unconscious in one of the 'sleep rooms'. This process lasted for sixteen hours per session and could go on for months, with various messages both negative and positive relayed to the sleeper. If one considers that a variant on this technique is currently practiced at a much lower level by the military during the basic training of recruits, where they are in many ways 'broken' then 'rebuilt' by their instructors, then like it or not, in this context the process normally produces the desired result. In the case of Cameron's guinea pigs, although there were (from his perspective) good results initially, the personality of the patient would eventually reassert itself over the imposed template. During the period immediately following the 'psychic driving', such was the emptiness created in their minds that the patients had to relearn such basic functions as how to use the toilet and even how to dress and feed themselves. While the process did work to some extent, as with the earlier results, it took too long and was ultimately unreliable, so something else had to be developed. With typical thoroughness, and not a little desperation, there were other projects running in parallel with Cameron's clandestine efforts; these were concerned with the possibility of direct control over the human brain at a distance.

The Onset of Control

If one considers that the brain is at its most basic an electro-chemical machine, albeit one of exquisite sophistication, then logically there should be a way of altering the electrical function by artificial means. One of the first attempts to directly influence the actions of a living organism was through the use of '*stimo-ceivers*'; these relatively crude implanted devices were created after a considerable amount of research during the 1950's by Dr Jose Delgado, a neurosurgeon who also held a professorship at Yale University. The classic example of their effectiveness involved Dr Delgado entering an enclosure with an adult bull that had been fitted with electrodes leading into specific centers in its brain.

The bull charged straight at the doctor who was armed with nothing more than a small transmitter. Delgado pressed a button on the transmitter and the bull came to a stop and stood, rather bemused, a few feet from him. This experiment this speaks volumes for both the confidence of the doctor and his faith in the reliability of the system. Delgado also experimented on monkeys, cats and human beings, until, in 1966, he came to the conclusion that human beings can be forced to act like robots and made to carry out actions involuntarily. It also became clear that the implanted person, or animal, could not override or disobey the transmitted instruction – there was no choice – and they became a virtual observer as their body carried out its task.

Other implant research was conducted independently at Harvard University by Drs. Sweet, Mark and Ervin, while at Tulane University, Dr Robert Heath implanted a pleasure centre in the brain of a young human male, and control of the transmission signal was given to the subject. He went on to stimulate this centre more than 1,500 times in a three hour period and, despite his spirited protests, had to be 'switched off' for his own safety. In a prime example of art imitating real life, there was a science fiction story that involved people called 'wireheads', who had illegally received electrodes implanted directly into their pleasure centers. These were accessed via a plug fitted on their scalp and in a direct similarity with drug addicts they needed a regular 'fix', and, also like addicts, could overdose and die – but in this case of pleasure. In the story, the siren call of an unlimited input of pleasure and ecstasy, in its original meaning, took absolute precedence over basic requirements to sustain life; nothing changes, it just updates. In another example of art imitating life, a 1954 film entitled, *'The Creature with the Atom Brain'* written by the legendary and influential author, Curt Siodmak, depicted human beings who had been implanted with unlikely and rather large 'atom brains' that allowed them to be controlled while transmitting an image of their whereabouts to an operator. I suppose another analogy of life imitating art could be made with the operators of UAV's and UCAV's as they survey the war zone in hostile areas.

Works of fiction aside, irrespective of how perceptive, it was now well established that the system worked, but there was still much work to be done on mapping specific areas of the brain, what they did and how they could be influenced. This lead to a rather gruesome project devised by Dr John Lilly of inserting more than 150 short sections of hypodermic needle, each the thickness of the skull bone, into the cranium of a test subject, the short lengths of needle acted as guides for the electrodes as they were inserted into the brain tissue. This lead to the creation of an electrode matrix that could be activated in any number of patterns to induce a near infinite number of emotional and physical responses. Again the system worked, but it was still unwieldy and cumbersome, and the subject was still wired to the apparatus.

Independent Implants

It is at this point the picture begins to cloud over: while there is continuing overt development of implants in the public sector dealing with, e.g. the fight against some kinds of blindness by feeding images directly into the brains of blind people, or sound to the brains of the profoundly deaf, there is also the clandestine research conducted under the cloak of ever available 'black budgets'. It is to this research that we now turn our gaze, for it is here that the really worrying developments are taking place. Now that the science of microelectronics is commonplace and well understood, the need for crude wires accessing the brain through the skull via hypodermic needle guides has vanished.

All that is needed now is one operation to fit a processor directly into the brain, a circuit that is activated externally and control established. One application of this idea was suggested in the last decade of the 20th century in the form of the so-called '*Soulcatcher Chip*'. The concept involved inserting a recording device into a living human brain at birth, or soon after, and removing it after the death of the recipient. The entire life of a person recorded in detail for posterity and possibly downloaded into a memory bank or even another body. A type of immortality at a price, but as far as is known this idea was only a hypothesis on a scientific wish list and never came to fruition…or so we are told.

The range of obviously artificial implants, viz. the ones that actually look like tiny circuits and electronic devices, is quite extensive; the only obvious common factor is that they are all small and seemingly developed in sophistication at the same rate as modern microelectronic technology, or at least the technology that is known about. It is obvious that early examples look similar to what can only be described as simple diodes encapsulated in a glass tube, although their function is a matter of speculation. Some are only a few millimeters in length and the same in cross section, and their construction appears relatively crude. Some look like the tiny toroidal transformers and tuning coils used in radio receivers and transmitters, which in this case might help define their purpose. The most recent are identical to the minute, modern circuits used in microprocessors. If one considers the processors used in computers, we find that at the heart of each one lies the actual mechanism, the rest of the device comprises connections and 'heat sinks' – this is what make it comparatively large in relation to the actual processor – and it is the physical size that is the major stumbling block to further development, that, and the unavoidable heat build up that affects its performance. This is not quite such an issue when inserted into the body, as by its very nature the human body tends to maintain and regulate its own temperature. It is these more complex devices that appear to be the ones designed to act as control units.

Conclusion

From their design they do not look like anything designed on another world, they are, in fact, quite pedestrian, and although functioning esoteric electronic devices, it is a fair bet that they were designed and implanted right here on Earth. This in a way brings us back full circle: we have to ask whether people are occasionally implanted with monitoring and control devices for reasons unknown, and the answer has to be yes, they appear to be. The sole point of divergence is, of course, who is doing the implantation and why? From the available evidence and judging by the composition and design of the implants removed so far, it looks as though they are derived entirely from earthly sources.

As already stated, those that are not configured as an obviously artificial device are composed of human tissue or small items of detritus that have punctured the skin at some stage. We are told that this is a cunning disguise concealing an advanced alien technology; perhaps it is, but it is more likely that it is not. The answer, as with the subject of Ufology itself, is still enigmatic, for any pro there is a con, one can only hope that at some point an answer will emerge; as was mentioned in the introduction, '*perhaps the aliens are closer than we think*'.

Chapter 36
The Politics of the UFO

The Background

The subject of UFO's and Ufology in general is one that gives rise to charges of the gravest heresy from those whose inclination is that there is only one possible answer to the enigma. UFO's are physical machines originating from other galaxies. Any refutation of this is viewed with the deepest suspicion and those who make it are heretics and therefore damned. The rationale behind these craft and the beings they carry has seen various incarnations, even the attitude of entire nations is reflected in this, therefore, serving as an object lesson to us all. Towards the finale of the classic 1950's Sci-Fi film, *The Day the Earth Stood Still,* in which an alien spacecraft lands in an American city park, the line of dialogue, *'Klaatu barada nicto',* uttered by the heroine saves the Earth. Incidentally, this film was remade and released in 2008 starring Keanu Reeves as Klaatu, the role first made famous by the actor, Michael Rennie.

By using this phrase from an alien language taught to her by the hero, an alien but human looking intergalactic ambassador named *'Klaatu',* the heroine instructs a robotic enforcer/bodyguard/policeman called *'Gort'* that, rather than systematically laying waste to the planet, to rescue and reanimate his by now dying charge, the ambassador. The film ends with an impassioned farewell speech delivered by the altruistic ET from the rim of the saucer immediately prior to his departure, earnestly pleading with us to abandon our aggressive tendencies, internecine rivalries, and most importantly the nuclear arms race, and live in harmony. The picture was very much of its era and made a point that was, in turn, derived from the bone-chilling paranoia and fear generated by the Cold War. It admirably demonstrated that if we cannot coerce, defeat or understand something, we must of necessity fear and if possible destroy it. Sadly, over time, and irrespective of how much we learn, very little changes except that we become even more proficient at killing one another.

One thing that sets the events depicted in the film apart from run of the mill accounts of other paranormal events – and make no mistake about it, Ufology is exactly that, a manifestation of the paranormal – was its malleability to the needs of government bodies. While this is especially true of the almost obsessive, labyrinthine secrecy of the military machine, it is also an accepted fact that the United Kingdom possesses, in spite of fervent claims to the contrary, one of the most secretive governments in the free world, but even within this ingrained culture of secrecy there are pockets of reticence that beggar belief. Even the much needed, recently introduced, and much vaunted British Freedom of Information (FOI) Act is currently being watered down to conceal the misdoings and incompetence of government ministers, and the sheer scale of waste and inefficiency that occurs within officialdom. The intense secrecy over the past and present (mis)deeds of the House of Windsor is yet another example of this mania for concealment. However, while all countries have secrets that, in the interests of national security, require to be kept under wraps, there are some 'secrets' that can be deliberately molded to serve a variety of purposes.

This is particularly true of the large-scale use of reported UFO sightings to conceal the development of very real, cutting-edge, weapons technology from a variety of sources. The worst offender was undoubtedly the government of the United States of America who concealed an entire generation of stealth aircraft from the public gaze by promoting, and to some extent encouraging, the belief in extraterrestrial spacecraft. The system was simple: drip-feed a subtle blend of half-truth and lies to gullible and credulous dupes then stand back and watch the disinformation solidify into hard facts – facts that had the dual benefit of discrediting both the reputations of the person promoting them and by implication, the entire subject of UFO research.

The American system of disinformation was repeatedly used to good effect on the Soviet Union, although in fairness they too were also masters of this arcane art, especially in the early days of the Cold War when they managed to convince the USA that they were far more advanced in their long-range, strategic bomber capability than they actually were. This of course caused the US government to channel prodigious sums of money into its arms-related space and weapons programs, which resulted in the first moon landing in 1969. Whether or not the moon landings actually took place is, for the present, of little consequence, neither is what was allegedly witnessed during the flight and the excursions on the surface of the moon. What is important is what was learned from it. We can only hope that the forthcoming manned mission to Mars capitalizes on the lessons learned and is successful, and that many of the enigmas associated with this most enigmatic planet are revealed...we can only hope!

The reason that manned space exploration projects were curtailed, and to a large extent still are, was not entirely due to a lack of funding, but, rather, for safety reasons. The flights leading up to, and including, the Apollo Project were horrendous affairs that imposed such intolerable levels of risk and danger upon the crews that they simply would not be countenanced now. However, at the time, for political expediency the safety fears were to a large extent either played down or brazenly denied. Among other factors it has been stated publicly that the level of computer technology used on board Apollo 11 was unreliable and technologically primitive. In fact it has now been admitted by those who were part of the space program at the time that the computers used, both on board the spacecraft and at mission control, were in fact 'data loggers', rather than what we now consider to be state-of-the-art computers almost capable of acting independently.

The Reality

From the acres of print created, the hundreds of books written, and the myriad theories espoused on the subject of Ufology and supposedly alien spacecraft, one thing in particular stands out: in spite of bold claims to the contrary, there is absolutely no consensus on their origin. Alternately attributed to paranormal, social and cultural phenomena and even visitors from other star systems and dimensions, just what they are or are not, is still, as always, open to conjecture. During the halcyon, heady days between the late 1950's and the early 1990's, the entire subject was a happy hunting ground for liars, charlatans and the deluded. However, to be fair, the subject is one that by its very nature readily lends itself to manipulation, not only by the lunatic fringe, but also, as we shall see, by official bodies too. Not least among the difficulties facing the genuine researcher is getting one basic fact across to the general public, and that is, a UFO is not necessarily an alien spacecraft crewed by extraterrestrials.

The average run of the mill reports on UFO's were, and still are, easily explained away through more prosaic reasons, viz. aircraft both civilian and military, satellites, meteors, stars, planets, temperature inversions, and to a large extent wishful thinking. There is, however, a harder core of sightings, both by the naked eye and on radar, which cannot be dismissed so easily, and a good number of these are almost certain to be very highly classified experimental aircraft. There is little percentage in getting excited about sightings of prototype aircraft since, other than personal satisfaction, all governments will resolutely deny all knowledge of them. Frankly, I would be surprised and disappointed if they did not. This instinctive, official denial may actually have some validity, since 'deep black' projects fielded by one country are unlikely to appear in official reports of even friendly powers; in fact the intelligence community may be genuinely unaware of them.

The rather curious type of mania of attempting to identify top secret military hardware also extends to the group of Ufologists who continually try to prove the existence of secret military underground bases; R.A.F Rudloe Manor is a prime, but by no means lone, example. The implication is usually that these bases are monitoring points to track the UFO's, not only across British air space, but also as part of a worldwide network. This is not surprising, of course there are secret underground bases, in fact it would be far more surprising if there were not. It may be uncomfortable, but in this increasingly paranoid world, these and other covert measures are necessary to maintain the national security of any given nation. Whether or not they are used to track and monitor UFO's, or anything else that invades our airspace, is a matter for speculation, but on balance I am reasonably sure that they are.

There is no intention to detract from the work already done researching these bases, but since the bases are manifestly there, and their existence will be continually and categorically denied, why don't the researchers involved in this subject turn their undoubted talents to ultimately more rewarding areas, the prime subject in this case being Ufology in its own right. Serious researchers in the field have had a largely uphill struggle to get themselves heard above the agendas of self-promoting grand-standers, media junkies and so called 'UFO experts', which is in itself a peculiar expression: what exactly is a 'UFO expert'? In spite of claims to the contrary there are no 'UFO experts', none! If there is no consensus, then how can there be experts? This is about as valid as someone calling themselves an expert on balloon farming on Venus. However, as long as there are tabloid newspapers and late night talk shows with a wad of cash to spend, and a desire to trivialize possibly important information, then self-styled 'UFO experts' will continue to appear and proliferate.

Fortunately, Ufology is not just confined to one particular geographical area or country, it is spread around the world; but the majority of sightings tend to be centered on areas of military activity. This is perhaps stating the obvious, but it is not exactly surprising given the nature of the clandestine projects carried out there. The main problem here is attempting to tell the difference between covert military aircraft over-flying the base and alleged scrutiny by extraterrestrials. The grandfather of all military bases is of course the notorious Area 51, a part of the gargantuan Edwards Airforce Base, which incorporates the Groom Lake test range and covers an area about the size of Wales.

Unsurprisingly, the US Government still robustly denies the existence of the facility, although accounts of what has been seen in the skies above the air base are legion. Again we must remember what this base is all about, i.e. the testing of highly secret, prototype military aircraft, and as such a magnet for spies both human and (allegedly) alien. I must confess that I don't know why alien spies would want to keep an eye on our (in their terms) rather backward technology, whether cobbled up and back engineered from their wrecked craft or not. Surely if they did not wish their technology to be used by us then they should be more than able to mount a retrieval.

We as a species often fail to do ourselves justice in terms of our own capabilities. This may contribute to our willingness to attribute extraterrestrial origins to our own technology. It is also odd that for some reason we are apparently only interested in devising flying machines and not exploiting any of the other (and perhaps more useful) technologies, which these craft would presumably contain. There have been a few theories as regards what may or may not have been done in this field of 'adapted' technology: transistors, fiber optics, and stealth capabilities are a few of them, a plausible but disputed claim made in Major Donald Corso's non-fiction book, *The Day After Roswell.* While interesting, the book only serves to reinforce the idea that the natural inventiveness and ingenuity of the human race is limited. The type of maneuvers performed by these aircraft as described by eyewitnesses is evidently quite extraordinary. Whizzing around at breathtaking speed, pulling amazing high G turns, apparently stopping dead in the sky only to instantaneously race off in another direction in a manner that would leave the pilot either smeared like a bloody pulp over his cockpit, or with his internal organs irreparably damaged.

It is clear that even our own technology is capable of producing craft that perform well without the physical capabilities of a human pilot to fly them, and the only method of rectifying this situation would have to happen in one of two ways: (a), a means to remove all inertia from the occupant of the craft, or (b), to have the craft completely unmanned, in other words an Unmanned Aerial Vehicle, (UAV), or its immediate successor, an Unmanned Combat Aerial Vehicle (UCAV). From the information available it seems as if removing the inertia from a hypothetical pilot inside a high performance craft such as those reportedly observed would require a very much deeper understanding of the laws of physics than we have at present.

To prevent the death of the pilot, in addition to suitable protective clothing, a small cocoon of zero gravity or a 'damping field' of some kind would have to be created around the pilot. The closest things at present in normal airforce use are the so-called 'G-suits' worn routinely by fighter plots, which are designed to support specific muscle groups and prevent blood being drained from the brain into the extremities of the body. In addition to this, the pilots are also taught special breathing techniques and muscle control to use in conjunction with the protection afforded by the suits, and even then they experience the alarming effects of high G flight manoeuvres.

On the other hand, to have a pilotless vehicle would be much simpler, more efficient and considerably cheaper, since the technology already exists and is in relatively common usage. The wars in Afghanistan and Iraq, and to a lesser extent during the 1960's in Vietnam, regularly used unmanned craft for reconnaissance purposes. The craft are extremely useful, small, light, difficult to spot on radar and extremely difficult to shoot down, they are also fitted with a self-destruct facility to keep sensitive military technology out of the hands of an enemy. The UCAV's are slightly larger and designed to carry guided missiles and/or bombs; they have an advantage over dedicated missiles such as the *'Tomahawk Cruise'* and its variants in that they can remain on station for some time before discharging their payload, and, should it be necessary, return to base. In fact it has all the advantages of a manned aircraft without exposing the pilot to any danger, plus of course all the advantages of a vastly increased performance envelope. One example of the UCAV can be seen in the widely used 'Predator' variant on this design, which can either be used as a laser 'spotter' to call down 'smart bombs' that home in on the target pinpointed by laser beam, or the vehicle can also be fitted with its own bomb load and/or missiles.

In addition to Corso's book there are reports supposedly originating from 'whistle blowers' from with the US military and indeed from within NASA itself, although it can be argued that the two are one and the same. One recent claim originating from within NASA comes from Mr Clark McClelland, a retired Spacecraft Operator of 34 years service, who was responsible for the safety of many NASA missions beginning with the early Mercury capsules through the Apollo Missions and finishing with the International Space Station and Space Shuttle projects. The astonishing claims made by McClelland surpass even those allegedly made by the astronauts who landed on the moon. The technician claims that while on duty during a Space Shuttle flight in Kennedy Space Centre, he personally witnessed on his monitor the sight of an eight to nine foot tall extraterrestrial (ET) standing in the freight bay of the shuttle apparently in conversation with two astronauts who were tethered to the shuttle. This meeting was supposedly observed for a total of one minute and seven seconds. The vehicle that the being presumably arrived in was seen hanging motionless in space a short distance from the shuttle's main engine pods. He goes on to claim that during another mission one of his colleagues also witnessed this being, or another of identical appearance, *actually inside the shuttle's crew compartment.* Both of these missions were under the auspices of the Department of Defense, and correspondingly were Top Secret and under their protocols neither confirmed or denied.

Although the information released by McClelland is obviously of immense interest, the question still remains regarding whether or not any of this encounter was actually committed to videotape or DVD. It is a fair question to ask because during any given mission, most if not all of what goes on while astronauts are in space is constantly monitored for reference should anything go wrong with either the humans beings or the craft. In fact conversations between the Space Shuttle and Apollo crews and the Houston control room previously released by NASA for public consumption are full of 'bleeps' at the beginning and end of anything that is said. The 'bleeps' are a marker put in by the computers recording the calls to define the time of the conversation. Neither is it known what the conversations were about nor any of the details regarding the ET's. Was this due to the obsessive secrecy or simply because they never actually took place? If they did not take place why would McClelland run the risk of achieving both notoriety and derision of either NASA or the general public? Was this in the public interest or an example of disinformation, or are Corso and McClelland simply fantasists and liars?

Yet another alternative explanation to this is of course that what is actually being witnessed is the test flying of piloted vehicles, back engineered from genuine alien craft allegedly retrieved over the years from various crash sites in the USA and other countries. These 'black projects' have allegedly been going on since the 1940's in an attempt to utilize a technology that, at the time, was still far in advance of our own. Well, perhaps, but there are no clear examples of this; if it was the case why have we seen no evidence to support the theory? In the Gulf War and the ongoing conflict in Iraq, and elsewhere, there is technology aplenty: Patriot missiles, stealth fighters and bombers, spy satellites, everything in fact except some show of alien technology. In spite of claims to the contrary this could not have been kept hidden so effectively for so long; in fact today why keep it hidden at all? Or, as Major Corso infers, are there elements of alien technology present in the battlefield hardware already mentioned above? Are we to believe in all seriousness that our race, a relatively sophisticated and nominally civilized society couldn't handle the reality of beings from another planet being here with us? Are we so arrogant that we think that we are the only life forms in the entire universe? No, not arrogant perhaps, but almost certainly afraid, especially if we thought that the supposed race was technologically superior to us.

This also begs the question, superior in what way? Technologically, physically, mentally, spiritually, or a combination of these attributes? Human nature being what it is, in the event of a meeting there would be a period of uncertainty accompanied by the predictable rantings of religious fundamentalists and xenophobic minorities. It would of course rather depend on what the extraterrestrials looked like. Providing they were reasonably humanoid and not too alarming in appearance, (the 'Nordic' variety preferably), it is a fair assumption that they would be accepted fairly quickly. On the other hand, if they were not and resembled giant spiders or had waving tentacles, they would be assumed to represent a menace to the human race. This would probably involve a return to the paranoia expressed in sci-fi films over the years.

For example, *The Day the Earth Stood Still, The War of the Worlds* and *Independence Day.* All these films expressed different viewpoints: in *The War of the Worlds,* the evil tentacled aliens were eventually laid low by humble, terrestrial bacteria. In *The Day the Earth Stood Still,* as we saw earlier, the ignorance, fear and stupidity displayed by the population and military of (in this case) the USA, created havoc when friendly overtures on the part of the alien were misunderstood. He tried to demonstrate a gift and was shot for his pains. Finally, in *Independence Day,* we had a return to the sheer, tub-thumping, gung-ho heroics of yesteryear and the overthrow of an unpleasant alien species by the combined wiles and selfless heroism of a few brave men. Fiction? Yes, of course, but does this indicate a deep, instinctive and xenophobic reaction to a perceived threat, or is there a much more subtle agenda at work here, are we perhaps being prepared and acclimatized for something?

Perhaps the process of preparation has already begun with the steady introduction of the population to the idea of contact with another race (or races) using the medium of television and other outlets. It would make a lot of sense to do it by this method given the impact that television and the media in general have on our lives. If this were the case, to present the ET's as warlike or aloof would be a grave mistake, which is why the majority of modern blockbuster Sci-Fi films (with a few exceptions) tend to be more cerebral. Given time, I am sure that we would eventually come to accept their presence here and hopefully an atmosphere of mutual trust would soon develop.

Epilogue
What now?

In this book we have seen how the application of the word, 'heretic', can be applied to various people holding various beliefs; but in all cases it is the context from which the term is applied and who applies it that is vital. Who decides that someone is a heretic, who defines the rules that make the distinction possible? What is acceptable and what is not? It has often been said that history is written by the victors and so it has always been. The truth rather depends on which side you are on, for in war and strife, truth is always the first casualty. Lies become the truth and truth becomes the lie.

Frequently those who do cast the first stone are those whose own lives would not bear too close an inspection, and in the case of a spiritual interpretation of the world this is especially true. Perhaps the real reason for the charge of heresy to be leveled is a fear of change and any alteration to the established order. I am quite sure that in many instances there have been, and still are, people who genuinely believe their paradigm on any particular subject is the only possible option and they harbour real fears for the well-being of others who do not share it. They are therefore totally sincere in their charges, but equally they may also be absolutely wrong. In terms of science and technology the motive may simply be arrogance, pride and a flat refusal to listen to any evidence that contradicts their worldview. Does this mean that they, in their own way, are also damned for this intractable outlook? The answer to this question is most likely yes they are, due to their own sheer, narrow-minded intolerance and bigotry.

In the course of this book we have encountered various concepts and ideas that are by their very nature quite contrary to all conventional beliefs and standards, and as a result are heresies against the status quo; so to this extent those who support them are damned. We have also seen how the intelligence community can and will use all possible methods to reinforce their position and those of the countries they serve. It is typical of these agencies, who would quite happily dance with the devil himself to gain an advantage, that they lift, lay, and encourage loyalties as the mood suits. In fact 'dance with the devil' is precisely what they did and may well continue to do.

Typical of most of the subject matter set out in this book, much relies on the context and the killers and assassins who work for many agencies, especially in the USA, a country that sets great stores by religious belief yet sponsors political assassinations, can still find expedients in the Christian Bible to justify its actions. Incidentally, that is not a criticism; it merely demonstrates that pragmatism and expediency are designed to assuage a national conscience. The USA is of course by no means alone in this hypocrisy since an exact parallel can be found in the actions of fundamentalist Islamists who see no dichotomy with the injunction to murder unbelievers, yet still claim that their religion is one of peace.

The reader has seen many such opposites throughout the pages of this book, the use of magic in the hell of war; is this an example of using one malleable, indefinable power against the worst negativity that humanity can devise? We have also seen arguments suggesting that we did not spring into being at the whim of a magical Creator God to serve an unknowable purpose, but, instead, may have been either the result of external non-terrestrial (but not supernatural) influences, or the result of a series of chemical and electrical interactions. That said, neither explanation gives any clue as to why we are here. The Religionists will say, in all seriousness, that our sole purpose and function is to give praise to their God, but are reticent to explain why when presented with a range of anomalies. Also demonstrated is the likelihood that what are described as bright, shiny, New Age discoveries are nothing of the kind, but are only old unchanging truths repackaged for a different era.

The only difference may be that this time around they have found a wider audience and are more accessible simply because they no longer carry the threat of execution for those who choose to embrace them. However, they were heretical at the beginning, and as far as orthodoxy is concerned, they still are, simply because they do not fit a pattern and clearly demonstrate that humanity is the master of its own destiny. If our race is to grow and move forward, we must cast aside outmoded dogma and embrace a new set of values that might just preserve our heritage; it will not be easy for society to doggedly resist change, but it must be done before it is too late.

Sources, references and recommended further reading

Arthur C. Clarke's World of Strange Powers: by John Fairley & Simon Welfare, Pub 1985 by Book Club Associates (London). ISBN# CN 2799

The Physical Phenomena of Mysticism: by Fr Herbert Thurston SJ, pub

The Dark Gods: by Roberts and Gilbertson, pub 1985 by Granada ISBN 0-586-06233-5

The Occult Conspiracy: by Michael Howard, pub 1989 by Destiny Books ISBN 0-89281-251-6

The Wizard: by Alan Baker, pub 2003 by Edbury Press ISBN 009188912X

An Encyclopaedia of Occultism: by Lewis Spence, pub by Citadel Press ISBN 0-8065-1401-9

The Magical Arts: by Richard Cavendish, pub 1984 by Arkania ISBN 0-1401-9152-6

Lucifer Rising: by Gavin Baddeley, pub 1999 by Plexus, ISBN 0-85965-280-7

Dictionary of The Occult: by Andre Nataf, pub 1994 by Wordsworth Editions ISBN 1-85326-333-8

The Scole Experiment: by Grant and Jane Solomon, pub 2000 by Piatkus 0-7499-2105-6

Gateways to The Other World: by Philip Gardiner, pub 2007 by New Page Books ISBN 10:1-56414-925-0

Have a Nice Doomsday: by Nicholas Guyatt, pub 2007 Edbury Press, ISBN 9780091910877

The Radio Times Film and Video Guide: by Derek Winnert, pub 1994

by Hodder and Stoughton ISBN 0-340-57477-1

The Men Who Stare at Goats: by Jon Ronson, pub 2004 Picador, ISBN 0-330-37547-4

Secret Agent 666: by Richard Spence, pub 2008 by Feral House ISBN 978-1-932595-33-8

Secret and Suppressed II: ed Adam Parfrey & Kenn Thomas, pub Feral House, ISBN 978-1932595-35-2

Above Top Secret: by Jim Marrs, pub 2008 by The Disinformation Company Ltd. ISBN 978-1-934708-09-5

The Mammoth Book of Cover Up's: by Jon E Lewis pub 2009 by Robinson , ISBN 978-184529-608-7

The Secret History of The World: by Jonathon Black, pub 2007 by Quercus ISBN 978164724340.

New Scientist Vol. 200 #2680 page 48.

New Scientist Vol. 201 #2692 pages 5&27

www.wingmakers.com